AQUEDUCT

for Kari — w. respect
with thanks —
at the pause —
the drift —

Best Luck
+ WISHES
Roy
Lumsden —

OTHER BOOKS BY GERRY SHIKATANI

1988 — Selected Poems and Texts 1973-1988 (Aya Press, 1989)

The Book of Tree: a cottage journal (Underwhich Editions, 1987)

A Sparrow's Food (Coach House Press, 1984)

Our Nights in Perugia (No hPress, 1984)

Language:voice hitting the form (CURVD H&Z, 1982)

Paper Doors: an anthology of Japanese-Canadian poetry, co-edited
    with David Aylward (Coach House Press, 1981)

Ship Sands Island (Ganglia Press, 1978)

Haliburton (The Missing Link Press, 1975)

Barking of Dog (The Missing Link Press, 1973)

AQUEDUCT

Gerry Shikatani

The Mercury Press . Underwhich Editions . Wolsak and Wynn Publishers

Copyright © Gerry Shikatani 1996

All rights reserved

No part of this book may be reproduced or transmitted in any form, by any means, electronic or mechanical, without permission in writing from the publishers, except by a reviewer who may quote brief passages in a review.

Typeset in Palatino, printed in Canada by
The Coach House Printing Company, Toronto.

Cover design: Stanley Shikatani
Author's photograph: Steven Ross Smith

The publishers gratefully acknowledge support by the National Association of Japanese Canadians Cultural Development Fund, the Multiculturalism Programs of the Department of Canadian Heritage, the Canada Council, and the Ontario Arts Council.

The Mercury Press / Underwhich Editions / Wolsak and Wynn Publishers Ltd.

Canadian Cataloguing in Publication Data

Gerry Shikatani, 1950-
  Aqueduct

Poems.
ISBN 1-55128-032-9 (Mercury Press)
ISBN 0-919897-49-5 (Wolsak and Wynn)
ISBN 0-88658-093-5 (Underwhich)

I. Title

PS8587.H47A884 1996   C811'.54   C96-930283-5
PR9199.3.S54A884 1996

*behind
the da
rk*

fan

*the   wind
             brin
 gs   rumour*

THANKS

A work such as this would not have been possible without the generosity and help of many people during the years. The process from first writing to this publication ended up spanning over a decade. And once written, it lay suspended *souffle sans fin*. *Il s'agit d'un project fou, toujours impossible.* That it rests yet impossible. And then finally here, this book which is the cooperative effort of three different publishers.

I pronounce here, the family, always, who lend caring and support. My late mother Mitsuko Shikatani who, from her Toronto home, gave me many things both material and spiritual during the times I spent in Europe, not the least her love and steadfast regard. My brother Alan, my first teacher in things aesthetic and speculative. Generous siblings, Stan, Norma, June and Margaret and their families. Friend, and part of this family, Kimurasan. And my father, whose wisdom lingers, now twenty years since his passing.

C'est surtout pour Book III, écrit pendant mon séjour en Europe de 1984 à 1985, lorsque j'ai vécu à Paris, que je voudrais remercier plusieurs personnes. Book 3 owes its existence to friends and acquaintances of passage and permanence. En France et également en Angleterre, je fus fréquemment frappé par l'accueil et l'amitié de gens remarquables et sympathiques. And in 1987, when I did further drafts and editing of the texts of Books II and III, I was treated with equal kindness. The following were those who were of particular help, but there were others.

In England: Janine Mather in London; Laurie, Tamsin and Thomas A. Clark of Nailsworth; and Alison Shiriff and her sons Joe and Charlie in whose home in Wrentham I revised many of the texts set in England.

À Paris: Le Centre culturel canadien, notamment Helen Rodney et Yolande Lefèbvre; La Délégation de la province de l'Ontario; Jacques Rancourt; Tibor et Suzanne Papp; Marie-Rose Lefèvre; Bernard Heidsieck et Françoise Janicot; Diane Beaulieu d'Ivernois.

Dominique Farge, Paul Collins et Maria Rôques étaient toujours prêts à s'occuper de mes problèmes quotidiens.

Enfin, Muriel Mathon. Elle s'occupait régulièrement de chercher des logements pour mes séjours à Paris. Lorsque j'avais des problèmes temporaires d'hébergement, j' étais toujours bienvenu chez elle. Je n'oublie pas que j'ai bien passé l'été 1987 dans l'appartement de sa mère, Marie Mathon. Bien entendu, un accueil gentil et chaleureux.

Thanks are much due my editors, publishers, and fellow writers who have been faithful supporters and friends during my intermittent publishing forays. Beverley and Don Daurio (Mercury) who wanted to be part of *Aqueduct* ever since they got wind of it over ten years ago. Maria Jacobs and Heather Cadsby (Wolsak and Wynn) whose quiet care and respect through the years is most precious. Two indefatigable explorers at Underwhich — Paul Dutton, whose support comes sincerely and without compromise. Steven Ross Smith more than anybody kept this crazy manuscript in his heart and mind, and pushed, cajoled, and gave good direction to co-ordinate this meeting of three independent presses which was part of my vision and process. The texts too bear the imprint of his editorial wisdom.

I thank Mary di Michele and Lola Lemire Tostevin who gave advice on Book I. James Deahl whose unwavering support has been crucial to me. David Donnell, Roy Miki, and Robert Weaver.

My friend Rosalind Goss first led me to Europe and it is her tender voice which often echoes through Book II as co-traveller.

Chris Zelkovich, Jane Webb, Peter Geffen, and particularly Liz Primeau, friends and associates in my magazine work, kept me nourished in spirit and stomach.

Readers of past books know that my brother Stan appears as designer of the covers (and sometimes, texts). Needless to state what's beautiful as obvious in hand.

I thank Stan Bevington of Coach House Printing for his enduring insistence to book arts.

The Canada Council, the Department of External Affairs of Canada, the Ontario Arts Council, and the publishers who've supported me through the Writers' Reserve Programme, and the National Association of Japanese Canadians through their funding programmes gave me the much-needed financial means to pursue this project.

If I've forgotten anybody, my apologies — it has, after all, been over fifteen years since *Aqueduct* began to collect.

A few of the texts here have appeared in *Poetry Canada Review, Waves, What!, The Malahat, Paragraph, Dandelion, Industrial Sabotage, West Coast Line, The Capilano Review, Matrix, Rampike.*

And what enduring inspiration ...

John V. Hicks   Roy Kiyoōka   bpNichol   Phyllis Webb

Gerry Shikatani
Paris, February 1996

Table of Contents

BOOK I

21, RUE DES ROSIERS
(1979)

'There is as well, ...'   5
'... and I did not know ...'   6
'there among the corners of dust,'   7
'my fingers!'   8
'and each night'   9
Chapel   10
'the moon slivers'   11
'a young sister,'   12
'Le Midi'   14
'each day, painted'   16
'Le Marais, Paris'   17
'the whore.'   19
'what is it but the brittleness'   20
'who we are, say, when I look'   21
'Le Gascogne'   23
'Toronto, Canada — 1979-'   25
'the concrete steps ...'   27
'prawns, crayfish, lobsters'   29
'Here in the clatter'   30
'Barcelona, Spain'   31
'here, I am the artist'   32
'To be summoned by dark,'   34
'I was the only witness,   35
'he wanders—saunters—up'   37
'And now there is darkness ...'   39
'For they say the pain'   41

BOOK II

A TRAVELLER'S JOURNAL
(1982)

Flight: Geography   47
And 'Before Geography'   48

ENGLAND

Express   51
Walking Hawkshead to Coniston   52
We drive around   53
Coniston Path   55
We find the camera, Coniston   56
It is a restful drive, Jack   59
Try the latch, inscriptions   60
London-Paris   61

FRANCE

Paris, early July   67
On rue Buci   69
Hotel Quare Monge   70
In vogue   72
'Brash rue'   73
Castelnau-Montratier   74
'two butterflies rendez-'   76
'and so, he follows'   77
Postcards   78
Lullaby for Rosalind   80

SPAIN

Cadaques, Spain — July   87
'Cadaques'   89
Meal   91
A parked truck   93
A little square   94
'I turn the page.'   95
The three sounds   96
Yeast   97
Besalú   99
Ansia de Estatua   100

ITALY

Rome — July   103
Royal Bar   107
'Everything is so big, so overwhelming'   108
Discipline   111
A place   113
Piazza Navona   114
Found   115
Park Gallery   116
Taormina — July   118
'up eat through'   119
'It was where'   120
'Brioche taken with'   121
Climb   122
'To sharply define'   123
Tarantella singers   124
'We enter evening,'   125
Exterior façade   128
'The moon is the mark....'   132
The left nave   133
Sediment   134
Oil paint — Perugino   135

Perugino   136
'What face is it I follow,'   138
The astronomer   139
San Pietro   140
Choir loft   142
Secret: Two nights, Verona   143
'The new edition / no'   144
'(Verona)'   145

FRANCE

Paris — July 14   149
L'Écume   152
'and this scarf tied'   154
Fast clouds   155
'Explodes, a'   157

ENGLAND

'And I return, we'   161
'We open our binders' history'   163
In Sussex   166
Pevensey   168
'Even these woolly'   171
The Hardy country   172
Walk in Langton   173
Langton Matravers — July   174
'Up the curve of the street'   180
'Bath'   187
The dream of Bath   188
A Traveller's Guide to Bath   189
Bath fragment   190
'&'   191

New song   192
Tasting notes: Rockness Hill   193
Holiday in Europe: In retrospect   194

BOOK III

AQUEDUCT
(1984-87)

PARIS

Open palm, first memento   203
The tabac: It is for her   207
The kitchen   208
Maghrebins   209
Who fidgets   211
The bend   214
Transit   216
Twilight time   217
Notes on form: The Louvre   219
'wheat ...'   227
Head-carrier's announcements   228
Notes on writing and meals   230
Boy   231
A Paris museum   232
She: To begin with conjunction (end as sung)   235
Provoke   236
'O so kiss yes, ...'   237
Pale: A cuisine   239
The going for a walk around   240
>   241
Texte   242

Le temps 243
Contexte 243
L'Église de la Madeleine 244
Friendly message 245
Trio 246
The painted garden 248
Day: An architecture 249
Translation from the French 251
Paris 252
Arrow: Sketch of landscape 253
'It is always what's wanted, ...' 254
Cloisonné: The voice indicative 255
Utrillo 256
Paris: Night as sculptor 261
'December 6 — rue de Rivoli, ...' 262
Falling off, or the held 264
Movements in a formal landscape: The athletic 266
The Pont Neuf 268
The measured movements: The jeu de paume 269
Detour of a woman 275
Rue d'Alesia, 75014 Paris 276
The bridge 277
Thoughts on conventions of staging 279
On interior lighting 280
Des têtes espagnoles 281
The Baron Haussmann 284
'Love, you have scarred me...' 286
Study in form: The Louvre 287
Roma: 2 years ago 294
Some views of Paris 297
Christ est Pêcheur 302
Decorative 303
The post-impressionists 304
Porte d'Auteuil, Paris 16Arr. 306
Arles, an artistic concern 309

SPAIN

Alcazaar de San Juan   313
IV, Four   315
To Cordoba   316
Mezquita   317
5 . 2 . 85   319
Guadalquivir   322
The breakfast of Seneca   324
War and peace: The toreador   326
Romero de Torres Ta-Ta 1987   329
At 8:17 evening, in the Bodega Rafae   330
Song of speech   332
Song of prose   333
The newest of new dreams ...   334
Burning   337
The ash   339
This is about meditation   340
Who notes: A particular pronoun, a responsibility   342
The light insistence   344
Points of view: The garden   346
The Goya   350
Los Gallos: The deep disappointment of the sea   351
The Tapas   355
Infacility, tourist notes of Nerja   356
Parts of speech   358
The Prado: Signs, secrets and sacred objects   359
Calles   365
Two in Barcelona   368
Fugue in Figueras   370
In Cadaques   371
Cadaques (II)   372

ITALY

The white, the red, the blue   377
The pitch   378
Domenico   379
She: Tragedy set in Campania   380
The frame   381
Music of the two worlds: Abruzzo   383
Umbrian spring   285
Stoffa di Firenze   288

ENGLAND

Walk along the Wye   391
'Brockweir, Wales'   392
A cathedral square   394
'Gloucester'   396
Bibury wind   398
Cathedral Square   399
The British Museum: Preliminaries   400
As in snow or strategy ...   401
Merchant of Great Russell Street, London   402
Tense emergency   404
Rothko Rooms   405
Black or maroon / A sparrow's grey   406

ENDNOTES   408

BOOK I

21, RUE DES ROSIERS

(1979)

There is as well, that constant sound of pinball machines, the crisp response of hands as they work the mind, and the strong atmosphere of Brazilian coffee, brewed day after day after day. The clatter of hard leather-heeled shoes, high heels, an arch, a fleshy pale arc, the sound of, aroma of steamed hot drinks and rum grogs. Clatter of spoons. A cash register, coins. There is the spiral, or shadow of it, on the wall,

like a woman's diaphragm, the dark vault, men hungry after money, a place in history: bristling, humid, the salt-sour air, men loading trucks, languid banks of desire ... objects.

*

... and I did not know what was to happen. It began as some odd wish, a plan — I knew I had to leave, to give myself at least a chance. Inspiration came to me in transient waters, warm ponds where there was at least, faint movement: water-striders, mosquitoes hatching; then, still life: fruit placed in a bowl, a cliché of painted art. Nature dead, *nature morte*, they call it in French.

Oh look, these enclosed terraces. I see, can see unto the world, the handsome tree-lined boulevards. People placed so finite this stage before me, of cross-streets, intersections. Look how that one glances my way as she walks past. Where is she going? A student at the university, the nearby faculty, perhaps. So purposeful: but inside, on this side of these windows, I cannot hear their footsteps nor smell the dark exhaust of traffic, that scent of travel.

As if the path was laid out to me. What was I ... her lips. That hard rigid line, but as if seeing through this page to the one which follows in perfect sequence.

The way red blood pumps the arteries, sunlight covering this small table, my fingers warm. I am to follow the smell, the waiter's trailing ash, the detail of tree-lined boulevards like a tennis match, my eyes scan across, follow what this vista offers.

*

there among the corners of dust,
the bits of gray string,
the brown cockroach-stains by the sink,
where a crudely crumpled Le Figaro[1]
was turning yellow,
from notebooks and a few loose pages
four flights up
at 21, rue des Rosiers.

*

my fingers!
    the round firm paint-brush,
the pencils, the paints
each day laid out
in sharp light.

the sketches

paper. every morning,
   clear, the notions
clues,
palette.
cleared me.

*

a fine-ridged
white shell
clean but for
/light
/grains of sand
remain,

       in
the trouser pocket,

my hand.

*

and each night
I would watch her,
standing at my window
follow this whore
home with my eyes,
turning each step
the lamps out
until only remained
the echoes of her heels,

this was the way I painted.

SEGOVIA, SPAIN (FROM THE NOTEBOOK)

CHAPEL

no light penetrates
cool blue stones,
fissure, this morning heat.
young children, certainly not
more than 8 years)
light candles, prayers,
under the dark, the fading
painted Madonna
such quiet childish
eyes.
   yet, outside,
these same children, hand
-in-hand a laughter
to flame this sun.

Segovia! this town
clamours its fractured shine
beneath the sharp blue skies.
   the sketchbook burns
my fearful hands.

*

the moon slivers
my breast — clearly
a whiteness,
no word.

a whiteness,

       still, echoes
              traceable

   still, echoes
then, whose
source refuses:
    lungs
    mercury.

mimosas haunting
these sharp stone paths,
call
calle San Heridia

such the squeeze
of moon.

     my tongue, paints my
my paints, charcoal
sticks of hands, wrists,
eye.

yet my naked figure
only,   or pile of clothes,
without light.

*

a young sister,

    warmth
of laughter,
blood:

a tenuous fibre
blood their hearts,
stars connect.

      sister. 'Dear Jeanette,
this postcard
from the Plaza Generalissimo
Franco.' this postcard,
to the right
of his cup of espresso, demi-
tasse he writes,

    'Dear Jeanette'
demi-tasse, left hand
to the mouth, the mouth;
all sound squeezed out, dry,
waiting was all. what she
actually received, what was lost,
somewhere suspended maybe
somewhere
in the mails ...
in Spain, the mail,
a little unreliable
so what was written,
painted?

    like the corner left for stamps,
  his left hand demi-tasse, right
he writes.
some evidence.
 a mark.

LE MIDI

Dear Sir:

In answer to your recent request, we are unhappy to inform you that we no longer carry the types of brushes you wish. We ceased the manufacture of those lines several years ago. But in their place, we are advancing to you three free samples of those which have replaced the former, inferior models. We hope you enjoy them and wish you the best of painting pleasure and success with them.

*

At first the bright. white
sheets of paper and overhead
those stars; her hair fallen gaze
olive eyes, what taste in mouth?

Mistral, her hair ablaze,
blowing the grass
   that night; the grass
overtook me, gusts
I could not proceed
in darkness,
my sketchpad blew
 through the fields. my bicycle
 heaved into weeds;
and I stared
down:

   ancient Roman village
   in ruins.

*

*each day, painted
death with his fingers;
  the mark across his
forehead.   hung*

*the rows of olive trees,
the dry, the stiff smell
of ripe figs.*

*each day. one café
to another, seeking the
correct view for fleeting
memory, image. speaking /
the   bitter
demi-tasse drink
and then to the zinc
bars of wine.*

          *it wore on, inevitable,
claret,
olive trees, dry.
his forehead, a marked heat
of mercury, the smell of figs,
the fingers which touched
everything:*

(that blaze of sun)

*

LE MARAIS, PARIS

where we have to eat.
scrounge through the debris
/life's tints.

each morning I must
match the paper,
the canvas board,
 and measure the colour
as it cuts the plane.
mirror.   and my

sunlight streams
through the glass,
 window onto pocked floor.

we have to eat,
earn our keep
God, cut veins and splash
the dolour
to the audience.

they do not see,
each step I wander
the cobbles,
the maze of galleries
dirty cafés whose hands
impatiently move, my back
/my head need turn
away.

take this my portfolio,
and these cockroaches which
 escape my palms,
tubes of paint, squeezed.

squeeze.
on table,
the oil, the crusts

of morning, the debts
of night

also
(they starve)

*

the whore.

        (who I remember
the brass-plated room number '23'
the key attached by a little frayed string
to a piece of wood
who I
the whore
whose clicking leather heels
in the night
to the closing door

the closing door.

*

what is it but the brittleness
of the amber thorax of this
cockroach crawling upon the shelf
the brittleness of an empty page
the brittleness of the night
the brittleness of the moment's inspiration
the brittleness of the whore's back

a slowly spreading moan
of sharp clarity
on the echoes of her heels.

*

who we are, say, when I look
in this shop mirror. 'Yes, thank you
I will take this jacket.' the tweed
I know suits me well. or that leather
jacket there

— no, it is for another.
it is the last one remaining, and that fellow there
he'll undoubtedly take it. and he does
look better in it than I ever would.

to make pledges, to take transfers
on the bus, to change position, but
to know who we are. so comic,

every artist who paints in this square,
their ridiculous landscapes — reds too red
blues of dilettantes'
postcard skies. but then to
shop with my own clumsy lips, the foreigner's
language of hands,
to ask and point for crayons and
boards, to visit galleries
carrying that knowing glow.

      like the coins I pass them,
there are no differences. so I come,
call me artist, call me painter
who back home misses me?

      ... yes, the tweed looks right
it's the language of my hands,
the slope of the shoulders, these
coins which I pass them. my easel
beneath my arms,
I clutch this jacket, yes the
tweed one, which is me, at least
once, in the shop mirror.

*

LE GASCOGNE

from up above
from this heaving
path, over-grown grass,
stones which crumble
under weight of foot, off ridges
and walls, over
the fields; the ochre. this
wish, across — to say, yes,
one is part of,
understands the history of a river,
as it fed these villages.
these clay roofs
over the verdure. 'say
something'   (my notebook
    in my pocket)
a tangle of grass
where it could not move
(the bicycle
  left on the path,
chain disengaged, black
grease on my hands, clearly
all of it discernible. blue.

  a parchment
  a bit of colour, this landscape:
the wind's push at my eyes,
feed-line to cultivate
the heart. memory of sister
her hand briefly passed
under mine a touch
which once only the secret
a remembered hue under covers.

her skirt blows up
to her face: opened mouth
of surprise, taste,
     (it was like this)

and drifting across
these roofs,
these green fields.

*

TORONTO, CANADA — 1979-

a trunk reveals its
travels. labels
: London, Toulouse, Spoleto,
Wien, Cordoba, Nice, Firenze

and also, a trunk unclaimed,
a thrift-shop banality,
and also, blank, with no labels
whatsoever.

           a passport
full of stampings, etchings.
indeed, I found this.

a sheaf of expensive drawing
papers; drawings which do not
move but cast glances
upon landmarks. famous travelled
cities.
implicit quiverings, like smudged
fingerprints at corners
of parchment: inquiries to travel agents,
      correspondence to foreign consulates

these travels through the heart
as lotteries can mark
the languishing poor;
outline, that is all.
outline of places, real
on the papers, in order,

shadow of a hand,
light as it crosses
the globe.

*

the concrete steps where the men gather,
canes, berets, dusty gray suits, their hands
held behind their backs. or at this café
where the women sit (they have no drinks)
with knitting, long stretches of yarn from
baskets. odorous beer, oily air of curled,
fried sardines, and
I come here. paper. conté crayon.

but this light (what must I do?)
which spreads itself across the neat green terraces
fenced with bamboo, which slope
down to sea. the road curves from here around
the bend where washing blows
from rooftops. the sea tides washing in, and I
 am lost then, in a place content, such place
where I sit onlooker and mute and foreign, that
visitor's looking
at these lives, these figures, these bodies aging
by table and baby too in arms. do I paint then,
myself into the sun's
still life cast there over hills?
O the singing I say, within, in watching and moved
to this edge, but never crossing
nothing to do. conté's nothing.

The line.
if I look at his hands
move. move across, watch. across the table, might
I capture that slant, that desultory / dusk
moving, orange across the ridge of hills,
the scant trail of olive trees bending ivolescent
clouds, his hands are lined, holding
first this short stubby cigarette, this pen, and
the glass of beer (laughter)

                did I say, the sun? smoke and ink
in all the sea, my heart's sepia
filling with his graze of light
across again this table this point
in time, which takes my thought,
throat uh, to rush homeward
the brush, to answer all sight.

*

prawns, crayfish, lobsters
all arranged on a bed of crushed ice
in the window.
and still this unbearable heat.
there is no one. not even,
the eyes of the vendor. a cold
beer. some prawns — and their shells.
this sun, head burning,
sweat soaking through my shirt.
no one.

.

I am standing in front of
the mirror. I am naked.
my penis stiffened. do I hold
it? the sound of my landlady
on the dry wooden stairs.
the sweat in closed palms.

   /damn wood,
splinter. before this easel. the morning
is light, to say as do poets,
to elevate us all.   the night is what
moans closer, reminding

a flickering candle,

the sweat in closed palms,
I am looking
far away.

*

Here in the clatter
of the bar after 5.
After 5 o'clock the chrome
table. Glasses hung
over the bar. Bartender
to the faces across
the bar.
Hunched over backs
of those at the bar.
The rose light
the flavours of garlic,
pickles, cured ham
to cancel the word.

This word he named
I named in my breath as
paints, as canvas
as a lingering draught
of a room semi-remember
twilight when it came (her heels)
there is nothing when
the travel, the haunt
of bars, faces, lemon rind
overtake.
Cancelled 'the time'
slipping away from me
I need for my work
(her heels).

*

BARCELONA, SPAIN

the human heart, the folded white napkin. Dear God, I am forever in
Your grace, for even though the mind knows the brittle pain, we eat as
One. the human heart, the folded white napkin. for what we are about to
receive, take to make ourselves in the singularity of the Centre. the
human heart, the folded white napkin. for protection from the nether
sense of detachment, on this traverse from home, the familiar — across
to this continent where arches call out Your Beneficence. the nobility
of It. the human heart, the folded white napkin. Transcendent of hills
and marches. I eat. I eat. the lavish feast of You the Son in Mary.
Olive. Cypress Time is undone the One, in time. the human heart, the
folded white napkin. for what we are about to receive. the goodness O
Lord, in the hearts of everyone, even the wealthy, the pompous, the
deceivers in the clubs and bars, the cafés and straw markets. they sit
down at last, Lord, in death, the sign, mark across the forehead. to
eat in Your loving grace blessed You are in spring jasmine and poppies.
to eat. All served at last. the human heart, the folded white napkin.
the dark jacket of evening.

*

here, I am the artist

(paint in my mouth,
varnish, chemical, brandy.

and the blind (white cane
I covet)
asked me.   or did he quiver?

        his tickets, the lottery

paint.
or I who has created this possibility
this artist; paint.
a travel even, to disarm
my own temporal sign. pendulum,
 like a brush stroke,
the paint taste, returning
to rest in my mouth.
deliberate word, writing down profile,
arrangement   (touch up a shadow)
to cancel memory of taste?
close the file:

           and what then,
as I travel to 21,
rue des Rosiers (echo of my heels),
what I seek out (his breath) among
the corners of dust,
bit of gray string, *Le Figaro*.
The Paints.

     with what to
wash the chemical taste,
varnish, from breath the blind
or any wretch, poor, defeated.
leave not evidence
behind   (varnish,
chemical, brandy   the light

          blind,   in mouth;
travel of indeterminate
stops, cane,
I covet a sign possible,
possibly mine.

*

To be summoned by dark,
night robing my minutes
before sleep. I am warmed
by this, her darkness which
discloses even the floor. and yet,
half-eyed open, I live not for that
haunting, the soothing bar perfume
of her neck, but that steady
stream of light,
given off, freely such wind
firing from her pulsing
pale wrist.

*

I was the only witness,
  at the zinc bar,
 and turned back
/ the glass door (the
prix pilote menu)
of the café;
 the only witness and
there
and turning back and
there, the outdoor table
in the corner seated
(the feather in the hat
she seated there)
at the café on the boulevard
des Italiens, after once again
dinner at Le Drouot.

the glass door, the reflec-
tion, just turned,
then.
they said, killed instantly,

the cane was intact, the lottery tickets
 ignored on the pavement.
no other witnesses and
what could I say? I turned,
the prix pilote menu
and she at the table
(feather in the hat, the leather
of her heels)

the waiter insistent by and
above me, *'Oui, monsieur?'*

                'Un express,'
I routinely said.

*

he wanders—saunters—up
the rue St. Denis half
hidden a shyness half
hidden a cruel
desire half
hidden (image
want and not want).
words exchange through
doorways, lips he sees
the tangle of rope   (which
around her bare feet
half hidden, in shadow;
always the
sun's rise, heat
enrapturing desire's flaccid
street. the slick stockings
'click' tightened by her garters
tightened to his neck. this.
this. this.

image which his brush,
fingers cannot break from
in morning breaks,
sex sings best,

  'do you, do you?' stop.
  a nervous flick.
  'suck (words barely
tie his desire (he no
longer feeling his penis)
but the brush of her
startling perfume
 'do you?
how much?' (her heels)

              an open mouth, surprised
              or panting.   dark vault,
              arranging the still life,
              the plane of colour.

dark residue of the hand, cuticle
he walks the street
again, hope hidden
the tangle of rope
around her bare feet
the man he does not
want to be
but paints with
his single desire.

*

And now there is darkness and growth and
heart relentless in its strong accelerate beat
of dusk, the air of olive brine, frites,
couscous and tagines. and for him she lies there,
and his want to say, 'Say *ah*' a finger searching
 to pry open the walls, the dry walls
where the anxious tints on his brush laboriously
move.
curled, mollusc of eyes thinned to enclose
in hand. mussel, or the clam-tight image
he makes: here a leg, there a stained lip-glossy
mouth, here a fine hair from nipple. There an arm!
There a foot! There the salty hairs! Heart,
heart of palm, asparagus with fine farm butter, the snails
(curled!) and most of all most daily the brasserie lentils
with salt pork ribs and bacon.

past midnight he climbs high on himself still, even
more insistent the 'Say -*ah-*', reclines lone on spine,
fused Siamese with a black June bug,
smell of seawater, seaweed, the white milky plasms
of night, and washes of colours even oils
move easily over canvas and paper; and
at the work table lovely with dawn
penetrate through grease-splattered curtains, a vase
resplendent — carnations and cheap market lilies.
and too, pens, pencils, eraser, a pair of glasses;
a barely filled cup of coffee gone cold holds this,
just out of view:

black and yellow shape, cockroach
fallen in, swimming, so it seems,
round and round.

*

For they say the pain
is an Achilles' heel
(echo), everything in reference
to a feeling of omniscience,
an object, taste of her,
own, prison this mouth, contains
object, defining —
each day, men loading trucks,
hungry after money
the load of words,
describing   or paints spreading uncontrollably:
the hen and cock
set before contact, concentrate of humours
on the blank stain
of a page.

BOOK II

A TRAVELLER'S JOURNAL

(1982)

FLIGHT: GEOGRAPHY

my eyes fit
through a cloud's
 fist

over Outer
   & Inner

Hebrides

    of green mountain
   coast,

a moment. mist

a moment
repeated,

of a bird's-eye
view.

continuous, a map

with these fingers
holding black pen

a period in flight, a
moment repeating out
& in
a design
in time, in

the flurry of wings.

AND 'BEFORE GEOGRAPHY'

and.

clear

clean through
clouds

whistle, which

I'm through

it all through

and.

a moment,
clouded
in wings.

ENGLAND

EXPRESS

Inert bus~riding. seat
a frozen still
deserted e'en: of Manchester, city a
cigarette smoke,
butts   sweet milky tea near
a coach station. street
still life this transposing to
memory, a private
reference, which to all
readers leaves nothing even
a point to enter, making
my memoir fleet.

    but arc, hilt
on joined hip of reader,
like sickle or partial moon
we view, a cutting-edge
'twixt reminiscer's
reminiscence, and reader's
reading: a still living
journal in this bus jerk
of commonplace and common,
a village green England's
inherent
tinctured way.

WALKING HAWKSHEAD TO CONISTON

Footstep
of daffodils, rhododendron

a foot —
step of word,

arching
of mouth,
  inch, throws to silence,

here. a twitch to the heel,
farmhouse of slate
and gentle sheep
heard

tone
heard on roof
careful verb
in dale,
in gentler re-
pose

a judgment
still / a choice

a portmanteau
of dew.

WE DRIVE AROUND

We drive around. retired
parson Jack in lovely tattered,
beige cotton sports jacket
at the wheel & Agnes,
speaking of Wordsworth, easily
in the mouth
of schoolchildren:
the divotted earth, bordered,
fence, slate, stone,
drive around, the winding lake-road
 to Grasmere, to Wordsworth,
Dove Cottage: most of his
finest poems written here.

> how short he must have been.
> *darrk*, cool. a washstand.
> heavy stone. the cold storage.
> up the stairs turn here,
> there, which phrase we
> can catch. which snippet   (off
>   the beaten path) be recollected
>
> ah, the garden.
>
>
> and beyond the stile,
> walking these hills ...
> composing poems with the voice
> aloud ...
>   we mark this,

footpath to main road,
/car parked/
drive around.

    how short he must have been.
    his opened battered
    brown leather portmanteau
    searching it for smell, the delicate
    crumbling paper lining is delicious;
    it sits by the bedroom window.

CONISTON PATH

One phrase,
arched back
to crouch up

the stairs
a well-trodden path
is easy
the difficult way
to speak

of wild rhododendrons
to frame with focus
their climb so high.

WE FIND THE CAMERA, CONISTON

To carve out this
piece of land
by foot

path

through the gate
farmer's field,
Herdwick sheep
farmer's stone

slate

house, house
through thence
by foot

village

paved road
by hand

        'door / latch   s'

into the shop,
thence shop
window to window   o'

slate village
by foot
slate fences
lay square fields
to carve out

sun beating down
over   Coniston
Water, we

view down down
from Annie & her
son John's life:

morning, there's fat Cumbria pork sausage
browning in the pan,
a metal ring
shaping egg to a
penumbra-round
yolk. Annie's smooth
bare arms dextrous,
floral.

a dialect of
slate & building of
houses quick sure
-voiced John. and

then dark & the moon
come late. we make
a short path back
with John from ale
at the Sun Hotel:

    Ros' camera left,
      forgotten behind.

we return, a path anxious,
back. night dark & the moon
land carved up,
we return:

'Annie, John,
we've got the camera.'

IT IS A RESTFUL DRIVE, JACK

It is a restful drive,
Jack. winding country
lanes arched high with
climbing rhododendrons.

at Ruskin's House museum (pamphlets,
candles, china bric-a-brac, and the like),
Agnes
buys a bottle of *special* sherry
to open for lunch,
morning coffee outside all
of us cups raised
as toasting out to blue
Coniston Water & green
hills beyond.

   motoring
through tiny slate
villages, farmhouse
and barn, deep muddy sheepfield, the rain maybe, no
no rain it's

a restful drive, true to the course,
Jack, thank you Jack.

look here, a fish,
shark swimming in
the meadow grass.
really.

just there, look beyond
this barn. thank you Jack, cheers
Agnes,
the coffee cups
raised.

TRY THE LATCH, INSCRIPTIONS

Try the latch,

hill church,
Ambleside town.

weeds overgrow
simple flat gravestones,
read some inscriptions, on lips
move, we say

'Look at this one,' then, 'Look at this one.'
a bit peckish, too; lick the lips,
bite at the bit. *A Traveller's*

Itinerary, story
and diary mossy while

the old stonemasons,
deceased!

make a note of:

Ambleside town: not only
simple flat gravestones,
left by stonemasons: also
good coffee.

LONDON-PARIS

Try to remember what
it's like
(on this bus) I write now as if
remembering it
back home
in Toronto (this poem) these lines

out of / time we're
going to Paris.

Algerian bus driver
smokes furiously, (furiously) smokes
& smokes out of Victoria
Station through London.
Hard seats cramped legs,
but this a memory of
direction only like
a metal verb gassing towards
a name, 'Paris.'

    onto ferry,
    channel crossing,
    only direction,

this metal verb an arrow
on a name
'Paris.'

rock music fills from
the back, smoking furiously
Algerian

an American tourist's
nightmare boarding the
'This is the last
time we travel like this,
this is horrible, aw this
is horrible Mary, why
did we do this?'

shift my cramped legs,
the pen moves, it remembers
'p' (it begins to spell ...)
remembers sleeping,
over channel. remembers
beer-drinking Irish family.

Channel.

French Customs,
identity / baggage the transient
'a' (the pen moves ...)
on the bus, moving,
an arrow's memory is drawn ...
dawn, now dream
scene left behind

      furiously.

smoking furiously, Algerian
driver, transistor blaring
d.j. French

thick in travel's myth the one
after another iron balconies,
Paris café, dinner at Polidor
we move through
printed, written word, signs
through the suburbs
the arrow a verb
'r' (spelling ...)

descending 6 a.m.
Stalingrad bus terminal
in the 20th arrondissement

what

will happen to hap
less American tourist
here
rain beginning to fall
out with the plastic rain-
coats move
a Paris gray morning,
cafés just just breathing,
unstacking of chairs unstacking
of moods
walking into

now. Late night, Toronto,
two months past
a poem. A memory.
Move like an arrow.

FRANCE

PARIS, EARLY JULY

This page offers little else
except too busy the shopping
heart too busy again
to linger, look for the requisite
nagging traces:
              Hugo in Passy, Stein on rue de Fleurus
and spare me / the wash
   tumbles dry
Apollinaire
visits Montparnasse, a café
at La Coupole and then
fresh fresh shellfish from Brittany
arriving in the rain we have
belons, claires, clams and speciales;[2]
the piles of baskets, the pools of water
and the sea salt smell, pavement of
such predicted moments, movements of
o substances, the calories, the food!

breath exchange food,
food exchange breath!
(O-la!)
Roland Barthes, truly yes yes wings a-beat
hard on this page. landing signal,
carrier of,
this day. this is the day: pass, step,
walk around parked car.
car, Camus, a car accident he was killed
by, gingerly
step on street, drivers
seldom give way less time for thought,
souvenir, Parisien philosophy, literature
and myth of course
of course,

the TOWER at night: *'April in
Paris ...'* and sensible shoes
on rue de Passy, easy living
salons de thé and always moving,
moving what else dear? the merguez
frites the merguez streets, the signatures
of thought.
thinking, 'here.'
no! what comes to me singing
it's moving
romance
is langue of
no!

clean bowl. song. white
rice to my Japanese round head.
no! here. hear. no thing.
clickety-click

l'heure bleue (image)
postage stamps, post
cards, signatures spilling
yes the quick coffee.
writing. a receipt.

no talk,

almost;

no time, yes.

ON RUE BUCI

At bite, red juice
of raspberry tart
drips down:

        our appetites,
for a taste of fresh fruit. what
appetite is such languour,
nerve; our,
her wet fingertips,
stained and also of butter.

we look so much
at cuisine, that
appetite of reach and
choose, having
each other

it holds us this sweet
inches apart and even through
our clothes, biting.

this red pool
(between)
at our feet.

HOTEL SQUARE MONGE

Mr. and Mrs. Sakai
of Yokohama we greet
each day start
mornings *'O-hi-yo'* at a
table of croissants,
café au lait
    ou chocolat, o mouth's

Mr. and Mrs. Sakai
and I trade faces
across these tables scatter
shreds
of Japanese, English, French
our gestures filling
this a Buddha's
grin, *hie*! a taste of homey
shoyu.[2]

Our greetings
and graces move afoot, 'Where
you going today?'
'Ah, to Bois de Boulogne, ah to
St. Germain-des-prés.'

Our spirits
move wide-eyed touch
ever so often through
uh, bow   uh bow lower
into elevator uh
still lower and look even
the hotel keeper,
how low?

Mr. and Mrs. Sakai of Yokohama,
we part, we part our own Paris day
paths carrying within ourselves
myths of wear French beret,
into the streets, into our
privacies glorious
with language clanging
in our hearts.

IN VOGUE

Thigh of rue St. Denis; and
black. blonde,
  blonde
shows her garter-
belt strap

to me: 'deux cents francs, chérie!'

then switch:
my turquoise sweatshirt with
red zipper, inset on a slant,
from a St. Germain boutique
: fashion.

then change: we are
à table.
after farm chicken simmered
in garnet Chiroubles wine,
sit with glass of red wine
in this hand, right, pose as if
not click,
the camera's shutter
captive, beautiful

image,

or sad a happy equation =
a story told
and retold.

*

Brash rue
Clichy moves its high

hips.   as cine
flick and cabaret
whores' magic &
wide-mouthed, red-lipped trans-
vestites' bang
of hip and purse.
arms grabbed by sex-show hawkers,
hot deep-frying oil splashing
smell into the air.

3 a.m. still, the brasseries
spill their seafood, crated on ice
and raw on streets.

Across the river,
St. Michel's paper litter,
rough baguette sandwiches the fiery
harissa[4] squeezed over frites and scarlet beef sausages
/Greek sandwiches, aggressive fingers piling
the greasy meat, coins/
franc upon franc.
standing up, eating what comes
with refusals, thrum the prostate, the questions,
it's
this place,
buoyant dreams fish-tongued
and silent, biting hook
the grab,
this magic, dirty river.

CASTELNAU-MONTRATIER

The birds cry.
opened windows.
sunlight: his hand,
climbing road winding.
        stone walls dropping
into sand, grass, trees.

        it is a Sunday morning
he moves his right
hand across her smooth
bony back. a collection basket
winds through the mass
rows. a young girl reads
the morning's lesson.
impatiently, he looks about,
a statue of St. Antoine, the
creases in his pants why
he is here he's not sure
why his eyes cannot fix.

the young girl giggles
as she catches him staring.

the collection basket passes
by him, the creases in
his pants. he moves his
right hand smoothly across
her neck a road descends
winding. stone walls rise
into trees, grass, sand.
a woman returns to the window
to shake dust from a rug.

she closes the window
with a creamy right hand.
he climbs the road
under hot afternoon sun,
looks into the distance.
the crying of birds,
the sigh of a pebble
under his footstep.

*

two butterflies rendez-
vous   wing'd up
on rusted wire,
grid upon dry grass hills,
yellow, green.

        (a sharp decision
        a small car winding
        the road, small journey
        of sight.

        sharp,
travels, twice this mind's
focus, butterflied across
thought
takes flight.

*

and so, he follows
their wing'd
path.
over burnt clay rooftops
waxy cypress green,

over the gravel the
slight incline underfoot,
dust, weed, pebble discarded
chain and oil; and smooth wide stones
worn floors beneath
arches, beckon.

behind the green and white
checked cotton curtains, he is
peering, his hand
touches the rusted metal clasp, pale gray
wooden shutters, done and undone
/over and over, but now
only for a moment.

he is at dinner: cheese, tall amber flask
of beer, eyes wide open
but shuttered within his
moment, eyes
holding a dark pillow,
damp stone.

POSTCARDS

Each city, each
village offers the customary
rack of postcards. the rack
turns on its swivel, with each
hoping for the correct view.
the setting we have at least
imagined for the correct
memory.
perhaps they sit
in a smoky tabac, a confectionery,
somewhere which certainly does not
design its profits from the sale
of postcards. the colour
is perhaps not right, the scene
is old without being correctly
antique. an attempt exists to
articulate image as metaphor to
encapsulate the rhythm of the
oral landscape. the card must also
share an interest with the recipient,
like a voice, stretched across the
ocean, over the rooftops, through
the path. the rack turns, but with
a pained, creaky tweak. there is
one which looks proper, but upon
turning it over, it is of another place

and we are fooled, slightly perturbed
that we did not recognize this. by now,
the shopkeeper who has glanced to you
perhaps once before begins to look
impatient — after all, great profits do not
come from these cards.
it is perhaps a sideline to other
sales. but you have come here
for postcards. there are too, general
postcards, which perhaps generalize
a characteristic, either universal of
most places/perhaps of the region,
but not the town. a craftsman works
a potter's wheel: he is dressed appropriately
enough, but has this been a studio shot?
the minutes go by on the holiday,
rain begins to fall in sheets outside.
a choice is made, somewhat satisfactory,
even eminently so; or there is nothing,
perhaps a newspaper, a package of mints.
on leaving the shop, the rain subsides
a little, but nevertheless, the streets
are very wet, the air is damp and
you have no umbrella.

LULLABY FOR ROSALIND

What this candle holds
in its slender flame:
night shutters brought
together whisper
  muffled to-
  gether, a passage
  of consonants,

an embrace.

this house fills
each day to night,

fills with antique,

  a gold, dusty
  frame: certificate
  of a médecin from
  Barcelona. heavy armoires,
  sticking drawers,
  dusty women's coats
  fill the lungs

damp, forbidden
smells, high cracked, spidery
ceilings oh,
and dust again
scratch in throat,

the cold tile floors.

tawny framed photographs,
mother and father of Mme. Ducassé
who rents us this gîte,[5] and doors
unfold
to the terrace, wild flowers
              & the brusque, noisy
work of bees.

a sole candle

open

night sounds
measured by this
candle,
blown out
dark is
its key to early
   sun pounding
   sleeping shutters.

back and forth,
hooked, unhooked.
shutters

    red geraniums fill
    windows, the stone
    cavities are filled
    with wooden doors
    worn by dust, moped exhaust
    and the raised legs of dogs.

this candle roofs
a temple form
in prayer

the noiseless, taste
of living in
this turn of
the planet, the house.

each day we wonder
what to do & proceed to
move through speech, plan,
walk, food & drink,
  taking us through weeds, wheat,
  pebbles, barking dogs, slight hills,
  bicycles, shutters, clay roofs,
  a game of boules, suspicious eyes
  & a drink of some sort at
  Café des Sports — monsieur et madame patron
  greeting us without question.

here in this dark, a candle's
steady, streamy
hue, a weight
whose tune shapes
a constant release from
the night heart outwards

        & the village is silent
but for the clattering voices of World Cup Soccer
echoing the alleys with their electric know.

        but silent now,
        but wax light now,

& to support it,
increase it by the old lamp
with that light
switch —
... there,
brightens our room

: dusty framed photographs
 of Mme. Ducassé's parents
still so visible,
the walls white-painted

damp stone
for touching
/damp stone, cooler,
                for this night.

   Move off, on with a weight
the hard and soft consonants,
    move into sleep,
   eyes:

        the gîte

                Castelnau-
                Montratier

    sleep, shutters.

SPAIN

*

CADAQUES, SPAIN — JULY

A return

a blackness

over sea

/

wind gusts

from green mountains,

'want you'

the beaches moored with dark boats
the last waiters of evening
clearing damp terrace tables.
the starlit tables.
cusp of village curve of bay road,
cars' intermittent lights
follow the round, and
up sharp streets, white houses
now darkened   but flicker then
here turns —
   garlic, sardines,
nose and mouth, open.

'want you'

and just there, Port Lligat,
Salvador Dali, home, lunch
of caracoles, his hand
on beach, tendon and skin, the opened
shells of urchins, dark violet spines and
trickling blood. paint a stiff breeze,
 hat flies off ...

the night
 along the back of a small
blond cat,
searches the dank refuse stench.

And along the road, tourists fill the cafés which
fill this bay.

*

CADAQUES

When night
darkens,
here the snail
talks.

'Waitress,' (as she passes
briskly) 'please, a cortado';[6] low
tables, windows to sea;
jar of
olives and salted anchovies
upon the bar.

here, with the constant story of waves, measure
of nights. a final, story's
close; café shuts
an eye.
winds descend
long purple hills.

   the spell of boats, ringing,
rocking, moored in bay. headlights on this seafront,
this cusp, cars
turn sharp corners.

when the snail
talks we
clamber up
the alleys and
turn sharp corners:

cool stone walls, shut
stores, heads
moonlit
travel the hidden
sea.

snails crawl
under a tent.
tent walls flap
all night.

MEAL

Tin metals hang
in the heart; cool breeze
billowing tent of night.
across this camp, silver
moon flashes, swims. taste
of pearls discovered, that
unctuous cream of fins, muscle to muscle
the rubbing, friction of bone, flashlight
reflects suddenly the tent.

a night of snails, languish in
dark peppery gravy: a monstrous
eye floats among them.
I
am seen
: an outstretched hand.

this place of tin metals
tables, take
the sun's reflection.
long twines of garlic,
shattered shell of urchins,
my hands, hungry for sweet,
for their orange sea, clambering
over wet rocks.
inhale, and it enters sharply
a question
or has not
departed. voiceless. I am tang
where brine, sausages and yellow rice
fill all placid corners.

briny sepia-filled rooms
throw shrimp shells, green tomatoes
and in my ears TV, the soccer match
so loud. but the details
fuzz.

the flashlight, as if fingers —
the rocks; by handfuls

eyeless snails are
heaped from the sea

   and the night steams
a silvery meal
of light.

A PARKED TRUCK

BESALÚ — JULY

The dark alleys
and dim cool lamps
of night. through it
all —   and into the dusty
squares.

truck parked.
angled,

against the church.

a bat calls sweeping
with an icicle light

cat, slightly suspicious
scurries past
a heap of smoulders, its back or mine

half-moon, a period,
runs
through it all. where
it hangs
the night stead.
stream of dust, flowing
a black, the hourly bell, a
mirror.

A LITTLE SQUARE

Church, fountain stone,
bench, dust. past midnight
the square's answer
is one. from balcony
above, an infant cries,
the bamboo blinds
sway undrawn,
     here, the possibility
there
yellow light: four
corners, of balconies mark
this simmering emerging breath

border this dusty world.

weeds, grass break
through moon, the
spinning
   from the firm stone
cathedral walls,
silence the square
it makes replies
its own voice.

*

I turn the page.
the dot
explodes
slowly.

      Toronto,
cold, damp
winter, snow's light
fall.

 even in this Catalan heat
father's ashes
in sharp flight of sparrows.

THE THREE SOUNDS

A tiny insect
alights:

the revving ignition of a motorbike;
the chiming of the church bells,
   feeble and brief;
approaching the plaza, upon cobbles,
   woman's rigid leather heels

      close shutters,

: a tiny insect
 alights.

YEAST

Besalú   Besalú
stone
I've looked
all my life for.
the wine so
strong. seltzer
taken with it & still
undrinkable.

(our heads dug into
the heavy, musty
/
musty stone
of the streets of the
church of the bridge:
River! River!

we dig

our hands
into the bag, look
for brochure, the image.

a stone. the 10th
century; heavy,
weighty column light
broken afternoon on a gathered
damp document
  of language, monument.

wait a minute! so strong

this wine. stone. I said
looked all my life for. as years pass
this, growing:

a stone. the 10th
century; heavy
weighty column light, look
for brochure, the image.

broken afternoon. a gathered
damp document
   of language and

antique cotton smocks,
dirty hand-painted china,
old, a bit
refused, slightly wanted.
(and the shop woman who smelled
of hot sweat, slip's strap
fallen to arm)

the little cellophane
bags of azafran,
pears, fresh little pears
from the country. but stone
(the way stone arrives
to rest) we think. a monument.

night: a bat flaps its black
mousey wings across
the night, as I watch
her, as yet unmentioned
my love

I
watch her

sleep.

BESALÚ

intoxicating.
Besalú: that
accent over the 'u' we
heard it & asked which
not here, 'hmmm,' phrase-book,
over there, corner, dusty window
'hmm,' as Besa bus, bus
Besalú, accent, accent
yes the right station here
the bus, here's the ticket
cheap. this
Besalú bus driver
accents
over the 'u.'

ANSIA DE ESTATUA

DESIRE OF A STATUE, AFTER A TRANSLATION BY W.S. MERWIN
OF THE POEM BY FEDERICO GARCIA LORCA

tumour, or is it
rumour?

odour.
though nothing remains
but the door.

the dolour. the cold
colour. pale.
in the frantic magic
of life.

salt cod
and the real
suicide. salt
cod.

fear which leaves
these people invisible.
which never leaves
my house.

ITALY

ROME — JULY

No, not the Forum, Colosseum or
Capitoline Hill. the cars, sirens,
the broken glass constant
ground of hard traffic.
vicious, the city's corpus
matter populate.   we stand
sip espresso; stand with cups
of gelati.
each morning like this opens, look-out
of sentence captive
in stand-up bars.

near the Republica
a collision in quiet
Sunday traffic.

damn! I stop writing,
an accident.

windshield seems frozen for seconds,
then like crystals, drops
to road; young woman
flung from motorbike, to rise up 'shock' desperate
crying, her 'no direction' where,
blood streaming forehead to
cobbled road, tourist book describes an 'ancient
city, old capital.'

in parentheses, we are at the main
post office making a long-distance call
home to Toronto. this woman's blood
streaming a vapid burning wire even
into this part of our lives, that narrative
has no end or
closure, but tourists' eyes longing to see,
never escaping.

no, not the Forum, but this: what
out of dark portals and shadows
of this basilica, a young Filipino woman
come to Rome, there is
the figure or form of Jesus and this
kiss, this sensuous kiss, the feet
of Jesus when he died is the date
accepts she/her;
blood-stained mouth her
from burning feet, one of
pleasure, other
is pain's collision,
her belief. damn!

forgotten to close parentheses,
brace brackets
now upon us, a phone ringing
she is with us forever
her bloodied lips, her weeping,
motorbike helmet dangling
 in hand ...

we are thirsty, brace bracket
another day (now makes

how many?) cold sliced
watermelon; paperbacks; coconuts;
pizzas, all sold in street stalls, then,
now. Asians, Africans, who linger near
train station about whom
guidebook says, 'Beware'
and we want to recount afterwards, we
'enjoyed Rome' we closed the brackets
so tightly to selves, dotted the i's,
a cold pulpy lemon soft drink.

pickpockets 'Beware' the smart-traveller,
don't trust anybody — Asians, Africans
the guidebook we follow,
are followed by this Roman man
by romantic or the sweat-anxious
bravado to the Trevi, that play off
the seduction of dream or hard currency, women
travelling might hold, the women we all are
and fail to admit.

the Forum is before us;
a child drowns in the Tiber
our mouths almost bloody
with everyday food, the joke of it
says we are laughing it off
this blood and eating well — trattorias,
tavola caldas,
and concerto outdoors

to the thousands, Teresa de Sio
singing
like a spinning disc
the dervish speed
of recording what lies
as it turns
in the space,
we've left to bracket.

ROYAL BAR

Dark figures at tables
lights flushed out, power gone
in the middle of day, sweet tomatoes
perfume of veal browning in oil, rain falls,
and feet cool, damp, yet through, flash
its open doors

sparkle of fruits in crates: apples, figs,
oranges, pears, tomatoes, lemons. crystal:
there are dark figures, the evening
shapes, men standing who beat at the struggle
waiting hours throw forth
in daily incident. accident,

that energy's return to light
tides of a working day.

*

'Everything is so big, so overwhelming,'
she says. she paralysed, frantic,
tearful in the face of mad, relentless
traffic, this damning at Piazza Venezia.

I pull out, push on. 'Come on,
let's cross. C'mon, let's go.'
to incise ourselves with miles, there's accelerate
frantic hold of each other,
restless quiet, remorseless
resigned the best of souvenirs
: a car turns; a car stops, sea of oil burning
dry. no movement.

from the tensing sun, the deep breathless
pant of Piazza Venezia, under its wingèd horse,
its flight or pitched neigh,
we slip into the dark, descent full of shades,
pushed against steamy soaked shirts
rush of shoppers in advance
to evening, the swerve of fast inchless
buses,   ring bell
        get off
        wrong stop; quick

to blame each other, the long sultry walk, with the
dusk, dark melancholy of buildings,
brittle glass fragments and slivers
on the street, a siren far off.
ambulance?

and again the siren far off, or near he's
running, running, white life-saver
under arm, far off
crowds gather, and
across bridge, always the rapid, run dangerous
current, of the Tiber
'go with the flow.'

bus into Trastevere quarter, maze
of small streets, whole families, their cigarettes,
sitting out each night and the motorbikes weaving
madly through the cars, and the lamps, swallows, insects,
restaurants al fresco, fresh mozzarella, fresh giant
porcini mushrooms of the season, mineral water, counter,
windows, walk, turn, the river, heart, address, a
finger, turn back, and here, address, a finger, club
in Trastevere, hard cobbles, motorbikes, insects, a lamp,
lamps, bridge to Piazza, to another
monument, bus into Trastevere quarter, maze of
small streets, swallows and insect and hearts and address
can't find it, find it.

        across street, quick

moves.
moves   are safely by hand.
         take hand into I'm.
         o.k. me. come. this palm.
         to close. close in, too.
         now quick in. bus home
         close in, this palm mine,
         this time.

the night bus we want
out of Trastevere. we check the schedule.
gelati. fresh fruit. pizza of four tastes
four seasons, baked in wood-fire, al Trastevere
tables on the street. out of Trastevere.
foreign lives our strangers'
bodies intimate with the pages of guidebook sweat-pressed
together, the cool springs from minerals
in water, that fatigue falling as one
hand to hand body, knowing Piazza Venezia, that wingèd horse
reins yet more.

Tiber, its drowning current. no railing to protect.
'go with the flow.'
catch the last bus.
across, 'C'mon,'
I say,
palm inviting palm,
'take hand,
mine.'

DISCIPLINE

This arch over / 2000
years old:
what the sky takes away
is the time it takes away
is the time it wears away
the space
the time it takes
    to view it.

/   ,   .
   a   /
   / A hot sun over
the city,

bright / the dense
what sky takes
away from the arch
the sun does in proportion.
when the shadows fall
it takes away the arch
in proportion
when the rain comes
it takes away the arch
in proportion.

          (
y   yet to ever last,
the volume, here colosseum
fills to capacity, 2000 or more years,

the burning weight of stone.

A PLACE

      here,   the orb
         falls   through

        courtyard dark, perfumed
        and beyond

the inner balcony

     around the
     orb

        falls night

a sleep, a rented
          bed

           this night's
       word.

PIAZZA NAVONA

Four corners
(from which ever we enter)
make a place this shape
four possibilities.
four rivers flow here, as
sculpted fountain —
pissing, drinking, pouring
it all
the flow: merriment, pain, taste,
structures of plain thought
or truth,
four giants sculpted to capture
in flow bodily form
make a place, monument in square.

the Nile, Ganges, Danube
and Rio della Plata, this momentous, in stone
conceived
we do enter, visit here, can enjoin we can
breakfast here, shutter speed, measure
of focal point, as in reading glyphs or texts
to understand, we are yet, ones marked
by this, any location:

merriment, pain, taste,
truth, plain thought.

FOUND

at a glance and by chance,
a carved face, storm and sun-worn.

dust which leaves
in this grip, the flesh

and then, whom?

PARK GALLERY

Voice 1   Voice 2

This is where it
goes backwards the

flip back
into the journal where

we walk through Piazza del Populo
up through
Villa Borghese.

from up high,
four pairs   of columns
         ;
stairs of the Galeria Nazionale
d'Arte Moderna

and we are backed
backed up swallowed
into the park, the hot
dry sun, and which road
do we take? wrong. re-
trace, swallowed
walk back swallowed
into, by it, all of Roma
no bus all the way
we fall all the way backwards
into the heat and thirst.

Voice 1	Voice 2

Voice 1

later we rest at
a street pop stand
rest the feet

flip back into the journal
where we walk through Piazza

four pairs of columns stairs of the
backed

backed up swallowed

Magritte. Magritte e Surrealismo
at the Galeria Nazionale d'Arte Moderna
whose back to us, looking

his photo which he turns

his hand, right leg lifted
up, does a card trick
which we watch
but wait, the photo
is a set-up, no progression
of time, which is
framed is
voice buttoned-up
frozen
shut-up.   Shut up.

TAORMINA — JULY

Up eat through

to heart,
      Mount Etna's burning:

stone   fire   lava

and the dark hair falls   there is a thirst
o, slow olive passion, under
shirt and from such perch upon Taormina's theatre ruin
as this, the ritual, the ritual day draught with hot breeze
to night's arch,
crumbling stone to water comes,
comes this burning sac
the testes move,
a lava eats always in Etna's
shade.

*

up eat through

desire the resort, of golden,
human form, tanning holiday bodies,
sweat and creams, taste the milky distraction
Taormina's beach

to surface through
a passage sweet iridescent
marzipan, nuts, cracked ice,
sweet yeast buns

these too for wounds, commerce
the ancient stone boulders,
as Etna,
as human form.

*

It was where
 we pitched our tent, orange
nylon flapping with wind, perched
on rocky soil, view to the sea.
it was our retreat
at night. before we'd climb into village
for dinner,
we made way down
those rocks, the dusk light
hitting plain buildings of Naxos, beyond,
even they demanding the moment's
attention, such diary's retention: more than
any inked brush stroke, the rowing, rowing,
two fishermen taken gently alone, antimony glow
made thread, fine wet and light
let out by net.

*

Brioche taken with
icy granita[7] in morning, that shock,
chill in the morning stomach;
the littered, welcoming beach
at Naxos:
all these we tell
to family, friends on return,
desperate for vocabularies of taste and sight,
and only half-understood
a postcard's off-tone.
but for us, to hint to selves
or nod with phrase,
a setting and image — fishermen in Sicily —
together there is this sea.
we float on a net lyric, sentimental
with the capture of fine dusk light;
our lives in hinged passage,
both of us ringed
in that incendiary
heat of recall.

CLIMB

The climb of this bus, constant
up treacherous mountainside

a bird's-eye view over

a camera
to Mount Etna's
bleeding lava side.

a smell painful,
a burn. my back, a fire
black sweater, hair,
in sun;

ache disconnected
overpowering,

the hunt for taste

street after street.

*

To sharply define
the words by their drop
placement in stream: aqua deflection, inflection:
and by whose land
irrigated and like as
well, those who come mute,
to drink
on sun-cracked streets.

words now cherished, placed
wet into a chosen frame, a
structure of dry
conserves. the line is clear, lips to aqueduct,
these photos still wet
on pavement, against the fine dust.

TARANTELLA SINGERS

Up in the backstreets
where night hides the stairs and wine cafés
low tables and rubbish barrels
marked by light.
   discotheques empty
with that silence which disappoints, only
the solitary couples over drinks, we pass on
yet again, wandering this prelude, this moon's
half-month desire.

either the quiet, sombre alcove
concealed with its feed, or the crowd with
its exhibition of sweet ice-cream desserts,
menu of wish in the noisy maze through piazzas.
so many lire this and so many
that, the additions on a bill,
customary words to a waiter, legs crossed
properly enough.

here passes the nightly promenade,
well-dressed and securely made-up against
this thin edge of sand, dust of column
its capital. here, to sit bronzed
for this night, to sip and watch
from the café we rest with such salvo
such tincture, our own hands anxious
and content, fisted around the rope,
the arc pulling us away.

*

We enter evening,
a train headed north from Sicily,
the burden of heavy frame-packs
through tight hot corridors,
everyone standing, fanning
the sultry vegetal air.
we can't pass one way or
other, train moving, 'We have
reserved places, reserved numbers,'
a joke, in burning and sweat
'Where are they?' find the blessed
release,
'Just find anywhere,' any space
fresh, in moving cars, windows opened
in the fast and faster
the blast velocity shirt off
wet in the breeze

we enter night, night train
'Where are we now?' unknown space
the mapless (it's in the backpack) in
fixed constellation of clipped phrases or
thoughts translated from the whole
in part Italian
in part English
the space is that now with
two Sicilian young men
in compartment we share
we leaf together in a phrase book,
we are four corners eyes
to eyes, on the pages fingerprinted or
folded, fragment to complete

the whole picture in speech
the complements betwixt cultures
'Just find anywhere,' I'd sighed
windows wide open, shirt now back on
and wet in the breeze

we enter with eating,
bottles of mineral water
and stops into station,
hanging out the windows
to the vendors
wheeling their carts
icy water and pop.

and then to enter next morning
yet still with stops
into more stations,
bottles of mineral water
the vendors
their carts of morning's
first cappuccino and sweet soft buns.

unfolded map, its way
a linear route of tracks,
what time and fatigue make
cutting short the heart and plan.
Urbino, we'd felt. birthplace
of Raphael, for me, that Renaissance
name always unfolding
my route back to Grade 8,
a project for Art.

Urbino
slow train
slow
late, too late we fear
to change
at Pescara station, more vendors
the linear route how
we decide with the heart.

we enter the day full-blown
a train corridor again no where
to go, Urbino, Urbino
each station closer
each punctuating commas
of stop or delay.

a flurry of signs,
the language of all travel: passing hill-towns
of Umbria, perched in clear forests.
we suddenly comprehend such vocabulary of choice:
Urbino
a stiff voice we stuff into our packs,
we get off and then enter
the reliable connection,
our hearts now swung
we take this train
to Perugia.

EXTERIOR FAÇADE[8]
for Richard Truhlar

PERUGIA — JULY

To enter the Basilica
one passes through
a tree-lined road which
on a slight slope at
the beginning
of this road
rises. His hand is fixed
on a latch which
suggests a movement.
A mosaic tile barrier
shines, as the sun
once again appears, a column of beautiful
Greek marble,
surmounted by a cross. The following
words are engraved
on the pedestal: *VETERIS COE-
METERII FINES* (boundaries
of the old cemetery).

      The mosaic
tile appears from behind
his hand, his hand does suggest
a movement of the sun,
a sun almost globular
deposits into his
breath, he swallows again as the sun
the column, present in almost
all the incisions

of the 18th century, indicates
the boundaries of the cemetery
of which we have spoken
before
appears from behind
his hand, again his hand does
this time turn
away from the latch
instead replaces, fixes
a window into place deep
blue sky penetrates
eyes looking in and it also
reminds us.
It was where St. Ercolano, a bishop
of Perugia, was beheaded by
Totila, a king of the Goths
circa the mid 6th century.

   In 1799, the column
he now replaces
a window where and the sky
appears again azure and on
the frame, crumbling frame with an
inscription was destroyed
the frame, with an
inscription was destroyed
by a gunshot from the Rocca
Paolina, in the centre of
the city, the tree-lined road,
attending this time the shadow of the afternoon by now,
the hand on the latch where
the mosaic ends to
the exterior façade, which hides

the Basilica and the monastery
of the Benedicts. Now,

>this façade is
situated almost opposite to that Porta
San Pietro (which the visitor can see
turning back), his hand
at his own throat or
the latch, two structures with seemingly
the same features.
The façade consists of three
>arches
the sides are
>blind
and the central one is prolonged
but he cannot see what remains on the other side
of the mosaic-tiled wall and
the voice he hears is his own
in the vault: cannot see
and they are dominated
by a solid cornice and supported
by twin Doric-style pil(l)ars.

>Remains of the gunshot
are still distinguishable. Remains
distinguishable his hand
must be cold holding
the latch, in the frost on the whole, must be,
it appears
still, as if ready
well-proportioned and harmonious certainly
in the lines.

He backs away, down the road,
the tree-lined road and
catches a glance, his hand
replaces the window
the sky penetrates all the way
down the tree-lined road.
Such façade was constructed by Valentino
Martelli in 1614 and it was
to specify, the intention of the architect to raise it
another level above the actual
cornice.

And now, if the visitor is tired he might
rest awhile,
there is a rather ordinary bar beyond.
And now proceed, and now look
backward, the tree-lined road
it is well-proportioned, harmonious
to a line; the architectural project
was not carried out because
the bell tower would have been secluded.
But the intentions of Martelli's hands
remain forever evident, frost or dust, proportional
or harmonious in the summer light.
This is the end of the visit: postcards, slides and detailed
booklet; and also, candles available at the stand near the
West entrance. Exits to the right
and left, and they are unique.

*

The moon is the mark. mark across. across
the wires stretch (forehead)
betwixt two buildings, their walls
intimate, a crow alight
flight black to wire, electric — that night
with a pearl, ache's deep
echo,
through the alley walls — the moon is the mark,
portal glow for, the doorbell ringing,
and all the night's gay sounds, that piazza over there.
the abandoned and inviting
top of the stone stairs,
just there, always
a shiver.

THE LEFT NAVE

Disregarding the first paintings
which are by Gemignani and Appiani,
it is worthwhile to let our eyes
dwell upon the Pietà

whose limp delicate hands
dwell here, in those of others.
four heads of acceptance and repose
take haloed crown, and whose
flesh silky, almost
transparent is dying or in impending
doom, lift up
touch such flesh, where hand
falls to other hands,
innocent smile which crosses
your lips and licks at the feet,
for thirst, a thirst soothed
in drapery, the weight
of halo upon head, thus begins to bow forward,
then darkness enters the stage;

the scent of flowers remains, and as the doors,
opened, release not the switches
of designed light,
but look out to
Umbria's
forested hills.

SEDIMENT

Elegant mosaics, a pietà
form, naves, frescoes
and floor of marble,
deep in our hearts turn
still dust; fire
without longing or
turning to words — a friar's

    'Elegante, mosaici, pietà'

who speaks with
the sharpness, history
etched onto signs:
but fleetingly we wander past significance
allude to physical habit from bar
to bar, stepping into
those threads laid flat (for us)
now, moving among crowds, here,
escape is only by moonlit alleys, climbs and
descents which punctuate our private steps
as they've so with others
worn them too, the arteries' pump,
water, clean, smooth
that habit the undoing
of sediment.

OIL PAINT — PERUGINO

In this hollow room, a cat which is yelling,
a feeding chamber; feed me;
and Perugino who is thirsty, whose hand
tires after little more than
a couple of minutes.

 (the dusty air of hills,
   a brush he grasps)
moving the curtains (for sunlight), the time
elapses (for sunlight) and this
how the brain attacks, takes
on colour, taste, smell, the attached
orbs, a moon's magnetic
questions (feed me) / the stars are
arranged in his observation
his brain is shaped
in this hollow room before
and after sleep, when he observes
the families they
come out from Mass
and before
and after sleep 'The four seasons
must) in the arrangement of stars,' a demand
the brain's pressure woven tightly and finely
in gobelin tapestry on his eyes.
depiction of hunger and thirst;
and banquets, the setting of moon
and the retinue of stars
and the sable brush then flicks
or is it parchment? and oracle in a bone,
the curtains dance — flecks of flesh-hued oil paint,
a couple of minutes (a glaring hazy sky)
in this narrow before sleep overtakes: it is
Umbria unfolding his
unfolding.

PERUGINO

On entering the central nave,
look 'round and there
find on the wall
hanging, the scarred hands

or at the apse
(the darkness overwhelming)
    the strained mind feeling
in what he was thinking gilt in devising the scheme for
as curtains on windows — the need (Biblical
Passages)

    or the Pietà in the room, filling
the loft: a wish, the way all as hint expands

    every day, a friar sweeping,
    : dust in sunlight

the strained particular mind and
scarred hands of the artist did not
show the creation of a landscape
which participates in the drama;

'Better to leave, than this.' down the stairs
of the Corso, searching the old walls the lines
of washing, 'I am

without name, open a window
or look in (an open window?)'
the sun descending from above the walls
/places shaded
by these stones. an arch, over the
stairs (darkness sudden sun you know how
it temporally angles, a painting
faded in that arch) a woman
through this dust in the window, housewife
calls out, 'Uh? It is you — good morning, sir,'
she sweeps
she is, dinner simmers (by smell
you know it)
on the stove.

unknown,
footsteps beneath,

open
the shutters, you

your eyes blind with sunlight.

*

What face is it I follow,
waiting to see, turn round?
room after room of a
gallery looks at a painting
then to the next and next and
following looking at a painting then
to the next. she.
and the next
what face?
turn round room
after room the back of the
shoe the small pink calluses
at the heels, sliding off the shoe,
from the dangling shoe
heel fully exposed, was in the café then,
the shoes slipped on and off,
painting, painting after painting
looking, face.
/room after room/ callused heels eyes move sight of blind
                  sight unknowing the face
    /from the first painting
    /from the first room
room after
follow these
follow why into
painting. painting.
frame. frame. forgetting
the moment given,
the face disappears.

THE ASTRONOMER

A verb existed once was an autonomy
in the stars, thus giving it name, as legend, habit,
and ritual the kind, royal still kicking with
passion and intellect — clings a duchy, that vista
into groves and sunflower fields,
over
the plains, hills and fresh lake waters.
a verb in green Umbria;
a verb on the lips of painter Perugino.

and grammar then follows, the hidden
girders lodged a sweet stick —

    moonlight   the passing illuminations

steady upon fresh green hills and sombre stone walls
passaged with steps old women must climb by day,
with groceries in ponderous baskets
upon arms. o, such tiring continuity
moonlight is, cast over doorways,
doorbells; or with hollow clang of Duomo bells
on deserted squares, and there are squawking
caged birds. here, a territory and that action
it be made from,
this fell
from Perugino's, his
 astronomer's lips.

SAN PIETRO

Moving, breathing through
the dark robes, scented with must, wood,
myrrh: outline of golden light
a hand, wrist wavering, holds
the book and she holds
her child, her dark robe
a source, faint smile, the folds

      flesh,
   in the corner, faint speech is
teaching: angel,
youth crouch together,
the marble floor cold
on their bare feet.

      we walk in the
house of San Pietro, a friar unlocks for us
the sacristy:

     a dark monumental table
     over floor of blue majolica,

  this is the steady hand.

friar who leads us into
the hills, opens the balcony doors,
sweeping the floors, carries us
in his acts of Umbrian verbs,
moving the hands
of our deep-rooted clocks:

'All this,' he says, 'before
Columbus': we are grasped
by this breath, time-worn, the musty
household

breeze of the hills
through these opened doors.

afterword:

a glance backwards, carry on back, —
where we've entered
this house
through a cloister, a
Benedictine coenobium
20 granite cloisters, a small
doorway,   from where we've tread

down arched stairs, a tree-lined street.

CHOIR LOFT

hand-carved which
uplifted is

still

dark. wood.
blade flashing,
steel
breath, sheath
of desire
in word, carved

messengered by angels
unto birds with trumpet rise
and to the parish
of simple talk,
and pure, &
but threatened
by thought.

SECRET: TWO NIGHTS, VERONA[9]

Bridges

lives: two nights, lust
of family stories,
shut behind the closed wood
doors of homes,

scraps of paper blowing

in alleys,
we cross under these stars

and then, the soft wander
across the river
by bridge
Verona's

dark
  streets,

        they amorous wed

map of time,
  map of visit

  that coupling
to call love tide's

bridge O!

Lamplight

Her!

*

The new edition / no
the print does stop. the plan
we plan: the grid of
affections to reach

the map darkness hides
beneath our tongues

a bridge crosses
the retinal,
that romance,
lamplights
the night, the River Po
glows
for streets unknown.

(VERONA)

There remains one night
I cherish here.
dry throat
hotel room shutters I secure 'gainst
tomorrow's hot morning sun.

one night, this
a recollection three months
from this table at Trattoria Fontinina,
Recioto Amarone, chewy, bitter wine
is a sleep, wonderful; bucatini
in a sauce of sage, wild game; cookbooks lean
on a credenza shelf.

cherish, one night
is across the bridge of lights
across the River Po, its dark continent
content in a natural flow.
a night over the map's dividing lines eyes slip
from pink (the land) across to blue, that river,
three months from this
the night will hazily then strongly
descend and will appear in a brain's,
a heart's hand to finger paper vestige,
a receipt: Trattoria Fontinina
It will read, but never to land here
this night, never its stone or silence
with colon, the sign which will open
the shutters: the shutters:

I will wake the morrow
with words, the window shutters
does matter peeled back
to our room,
will allow that sun and the words will be
punctual, current and practical:
but, my Italian bad: for brioche and
the morning's first cappuccino; enquiry
as to size of jacket to a shop girl;
sizing up the departure times at Central Station,
leaving on that later train.

FRANCE

PARIS — JULY 14

We didn't know it was Bastille Day.
we did not know this city
so closed, so, to speak then,
fêted and strange — and this return,
our only day
a turn   too empty
we filled streets with desire
that want, to break shop windows
to have lights turned on
to be fitted, to hold new
objects with their fierce
shine of gold.

returning with expectation
leaves nothing in the streets
but the cold hand pressed
against hope arcing to
image, want: a mirror
of planned wants arranging
the city, a map
too simple.

even markets closed —
   the steel posts and frames for awnings,
the piled crates and peach skins wet
on stained concrete —
investigating menus of darkened
restaurants. the cold hand pressed
against the glass,
        'We can take those prices, eh?
This would have been good.'

>   too good: too image
>   a mirror: this city
> of right and left bank and the
> shimmering river. River.

But how this ceases
to be interesting, this return
to the city called Paris
ends with this, ends
with the word

'ends.'

O, how it lingers.

*

but gone. but gone

*

That pursuit of city in visit, to take it all quick,
breath,
all the passages;

the waste, one feels of time spent unwise, yet,
a steady light enters, cascades, streamy — a slow
fusilage, even arterial, nourishment through fast
and thick of car traffic;
pounding scales of hips and high heels.

it will come slow down, it will remain, it
can, the brittle second, so crystal, delicate
and precious in a watch
of sites.

passage those ways of location, venue, without rush,
in adherence hence, to light. Visit Paris like this.

L'ÉCUME
    for Elisabeth Caumont[10]

The voice implanted,
resonant smoke.   cellar-stone.
she, the figure of a voice
turning   in a cave,   l'Écume, une boite de jazz

    in tenor sax, a muted
    trumpet, her palate tongue
    'touches bass,' a swift
    of wrist-bangles
    is smoke, fuse to plucked string.

when we came back, months later
(bass rhythm
couldn't find that path,
the street, that door
or Elisabeth, chanteuse,
that table at the precise
corner of return.   that resonant
cave feel of cellar-stone where
we'd return cold hands,
clutching our coins
to Paris

      (her voice)
(her singing,   red-polished
  nails)
      that
her voice turning that
'Round Midnight, from desire
(the distant)

             a figure, it was
             her, she was
             that corner,

             precise note
of a city.

*

and this scarf tied
once just below neck,

again just,
a little lower.

   and this form
mute fashion,

      being to
action, this writing
 of sign, tied once here.
then a hand. mine,
wrapping it again,

  this way this
cloth enters this poem
on the thin edge
 of a line this word
or scarf which
knots the desire
of breath
into the hand.

writing this passion
into the respirate
world.

FAST CLOUDS

A sweater
so large,
I put

commercial want

pass and pass
boutiques

    this
passion, fast clouds

then showers
then sunlight
afternoon or dusk
that light
upon river

such fast clouds,

something,

how to write
to jot and jog

that contact,

fit

so large

the crisp,
sweet melting butter,
omelette a myth

that fast plate
of shimmering.

*

Explodes, a
package, taste yet
another night,

an overnight
ferry-boat sailing
the Channel to
England.

upon my tongue is
wetness drying,
a developing print
of recall I want it fixed.

'An express, m'sieur,'
pay francs, certainly the French music on the radio,
just an image, that wallet souvenir
this boat pushing out of
French seas.

it explodes; this a dot,
the brilliant white light
burning with precision,
pulling at the corners
of my mouth.

ENGLAND

*

And I return, we
return to-
gether, the full of silence
in train to night-ferry
at Dieppe, the waiting overnight, restless,
in the dull chairs, cruel jibes, we
gather selves back to-
gether,
back to Britain.

and here, with her mother and Aunt Betty who
retrieve us by car, holding back
then, complaints hidden
from them and look:

    ready the camera, and shoot,

    in front of the Tiger Inn,
    East Deane: me
    b'tween her mother Pat
    and Betty. ah,
    umbrella tells
    the weather.

and here, the village green, count
through generations, page after page
Victorian chapters describe this same,
village green hail
Green England, and too the grey warm it
hangs in Sussex.

this wet grass: this gravel path
splitting in two
to the Tiger Inn, to
parish church.

    sleeping yard, we wander
count through grey tablets,
moss-covered, together
this embrace is it pleasant death then (?)

'Can you make out this name and date?'
I ask her. pleasant death is such forget

the climate, describe emotions, the topography
on ordnance map say, too, we are together, or a gather
of so many hard and cool modifiers pushing subject against
predicate, the circular paths we pile in front and back
with passion or affection, this kind of travelling of
arriving and leaving, catching trains and leaving boats,
we are tourists and strangers with eye-flickering nerves
our breaths the edges of insult or flint.

*

We open our binders' history
into this field where her Grandma stumbles
her trodding feet still fired by
desire's wit, a curled wrinkled hand waving
yes and no says life death over
ninety years her eyes shine
with unsure judgment, the golden
jewel of belief.

scalp's thinned,
white scrawls, her hair,
her stare.
stare again and eating clumsily,
crumbs or unspoken words, take eventuality
to hospital and death.
She. Ros. Pat. Betty. Connie
her companion, her maid answers
her every knock on wall, her
child's attention.

   in this house:
   New Upperton Rd. together

these biscuits ...

a tea ...
     close the iron gate open
the door, enter this house New Upperton Rd. this
is the family remembered: Pat. Betty ...
the low faint hum is always,
a photo last year's or was it
three years,
in the pile of Sunday papers, today's
photo in colour,

or the smell of food
it's gone musty from a house
the lineage, a
direction.

*

What winds which gust
from Beachy Head Inn, the chalk cliffs

white to the grand façades of bleached
and pink resort hotels, vacancy or not signs
here the edge to the sea, from the grand
promenade ring to the corner cafeteria
& chip shop, the teas, the tunes gentle
military bands play.

plastic cagoule, the wind-tossed volumes,
or creased beige poplin, a sturdy
snug-fitting cap;

a fag, smoke rings in air
that nicotine smell,
someone on holiday.

and with her this walk, across
this blank drop to sea, inter-
mittent with signs, a speech she grasps
it's chalk and salt
in hand the memory dampers, of
childhood visits,
the crumpled wrapper of Wall's ice cream
she nostalgically eats,

this plainsong blur
image clear in her heart
it burrs.

squeeze, in a sponge
the absorption. squeeze
is always the tight-fist
of breath, the 'I'm
losing my breath,' she feels
squeeze in the palm the paper wrapper,
the words on packaging, that history
a bit of ice cream and chocolate
it still stains sticky
the fingers and it's
garbage, look for a rubbish bin
to throw it away, have to hold it
awhile, it's
all garbage,

'How much did the Wall's ice cream
cost?' I ask her.

IN SUSSEX

Built well
in the English style:
Georgian, early Gothic, the Celtic
hold, even.
memory upon memory,
stone upon stone
upon build it each
we well.

a light, warm within
a white-painted pub,
that heart pulses forward
to walking Eastbourne Beach, up
to High Street, past
the neat holiday B&B's
built upon
memory to memory juxtapose,
'heart of this matter'
what we build of myth
a structure,
how we find names
in breath in the
movements of each day:
fresh-cut sandwiches,
stale feeble coffee poured
from an urn; tea shops, tins of shandy;
schoolgirls with short-cropped hair
& minis (the woman pulling
    shopping buggy glances over
    shoulder; we are caught
      slight in the time's eye
        like a quick figure,
          gesture of speech) Poomp!

or groups of Italian schoolgirls
here for summer
to speak English

all the High Street
comes settle down
the hollow, walk towards home,
cradled even where
memory upon
memory, stone upon
stone, do we point
towards home: Georgian,
early Gothic, the Celtic
even, built well
what we do
each day. fixed
in plot
O Sussex.

PEVENSEY

Sheep at Pevensey

Sky at Pevensey
Castle
    sheep at
                                            car
    sheep at
Pevensey
                                              drive to
Beachy Head
                              sheep at
Beachy Head pub   Pat, Betty,
Ros and I

                            sheep at
crisps   smoky bacon flavour
    local bitter again
sheep   at Pevensey
    or ale, this time

                            sheep

driving past the façades of grand hotels
sheep sheep.
        Eastbourne
              sheep-sheep.

                              Pevensey Castle at
                         dusk-sheep
grazing sheep at
grazing green

                         fence / sky

                 measure the land walk the sky
ancients
                                             touring in a car
sheep   touring Eastbourne environs
                         sheep at

kid's prick   sheep   or
take a picture   poses   kid's prick
'hey!'   sheep at Pevensey hey
                         Pevensey hey Pevensey hey!
'Hey, take my picture, my prick.'

                    sheep.
the Old stone remains. tiny stones.

sheep   sheep.
stone upon little
                    stones upon   marked, dried together
form an archway to the pub.

                        Pevensey
                            arch bicuspid
        sky
sheep at

Indian take-away I'm hungry

                        sheep at

papadams, gobi aloo

to take away

sheep   sheep

take away back home

New Upperton Rd.

take away Indian
food
                back home
sheep
                back home

gobi aloo dusk — sheep grazing,
grazing green the evening.

take away,
                    come back
    sheep.

*

Even these woolly
Perbick sheep
spied through a railing, a stone-
assembled fence.   our paths do cross,
the sheep who ride
the bus to Poole.
sheep's
the white fluff, and grazing
or chatting, away, yeah,
with the coach-station punkers,
or yeah, those young Italian schoolgirls
wearing their bright shetlands:
   'Nice pullovers you've got there,'
it's overheard of sheep and
they chat to a coach driver,
he says, 'This is more like summer,
luv. And 'bout time. 60p ...' crank
the usual, ring, winds the ticket machine,
a stub;

sheep chat
whatever. pint at the local,
'No need for the election, but, that's just us,'
they opine,

sweet smell of fire, barley, graze, loll in
furry coats and all
Perbick sun the daylong,
we cross the gate, follow them Dorset
across pasture, here they've fallen
to quiet, heads perked up
to the seawinds'
sunny blast.

THE HARDY COUNTRY

thought   turning
the word   'magic'

   sours

      /kept to
footsteps both
of us follow

                path
cut the green land
eyes which take
in the scale of stone
fences,   all to sea.

seacoast, sun's scope
all, to see green
brings energy back
in winds. honey down
the granary bread, treeless
sight and
the living matter in rock-pools
at sea, all goes there to
a tuney silence, after
thought,   or so,
to speak.

WALK IN LANGTON

counting sheep, bedside
alarm. tick-tick
sudden sweat's
ring of night.

plaintive song:

on the hill
of Langton
in Dorset by sea,

a sheaf of fine sheep,
see. eye to eye
meet.
taste of supper
to the table, a joint
a chop of meat
fresh mint is cut.
a sheaf of fine sheep
we turn the pages
up the path, foot
by foot, thinking
of blood on a fine
sunny day. foot
by foot this path
like Perbick rock
our joy imbeds
with tear.

LANGTON MATRAVERS — JULY

And so, Kate,
we've come here:
 smell of fish
'n' chips, hands
grease 'n' vinegar
lingering

in the coach.

come atop the world, in dusk
arrive by bus.
your Dorset home
Kate, where farm hearts
this village: Langton. stop.
Langton Matravers, stop. built-
all of Perbick stone,
as you said in Toronto
all Perbick names
you have given us: Mark
and Janet Haver. 'A one-pub
town,' you reminisced
on the phone and 'Good
pub food.' we trace
such journal saved under
your tongue what our tongues
reveal this Dorset

'She went to Canada,'
that Kate Woods, 'now Kent,'
we tell, seek out by
naming such things to
ring clear in this
air risen high over
green pastures to breaking
sea. but here
your story is what names
us too, come to Langton how
we are named by
a placement, situ-
ating in visit which needlepoint
threads,
the spun moments
of your heart.

between Corfe Castle and Swanage
we bring the name
Kate Woods, connect
our packs laid down
in King's Arms, the grey
fossilized stones;
between Corfe Castle and Swanage
we bring the name
Knitson Farm

from here, over that way
into the hills is Knitson
and Kitchie House
bringing back name
grew up here at Knitson
'Ah, Katja,' one says:
a music school your mother
once ran at Knitson;

between Corfe Castle, Swanage
a one-road town Langton
Matravers

and in this pub
a woman trying to —
             'Kate Woods? No, I can't say
I recall.
But Knitson Farm is out back there, between
Corfe, Swanage.'

recall in the earth,
the land, the years
of construction, road paving the blackstuff,
whitewashing, fossils in
tense, imbedded in their stone.

                    recall is the
name we have
in this tight stone-wrought
pub. smooth-worn bench,
chatter, pint
by half-pint, reassurance
in greetings to farewells
wear the wide-stone floors.

  land the years,
worn through
the construction of settlement
and home, Kate
the shift into memory

she walked on this road,
she walked on this road,
the hard paving which gives under
the access of a name.

'And Gerry, there was
also Studland Beach,'

from across the height
look out to Isle of Wight;
trail over chalk down
said 'A good pub
in Studland,'
Kate's voice still
on the line.

what foot picks
up of chalk the residue
and metal rail, that path
and stone and yellow
breeze, brief forget-me-nots
look to those fading hills,
the night in a shake,
brews clouded,
night's call.

cold manure, stone.
memory, rail we walk,
mesmerized thought: this dark
road we trail
    before and now after
simple pub dinner:
salad cream, pickled onions.

the purple cool
air of Langton,
to take us home
to sleep.

B&B's sausage 'n' eggs,
tea, cool toast in the rack
what Mrs. How serves;
and she says
the food she once cooked
for the students
at your mother's school, when
flutes, cellos
charmed pastures and stiles at
Knitson Farm.

there is a face
we will attach to the
land, Janet at Knitson door,
greeting us, unannounced faces of strangers.

'What will they think?'
we'd wondered together,
walking up at lunchtime,
looking for the Havers — Mark
and Janet

  /knock-knock here
is the fresh gooseberry
jam the fresh raspberry
jam, a wedge of cheese,
a glass of fresh raw milk,
invited around a table.

we deliver your name
with a foreign stamp, Kate, but
such integer shared in telling
of you as child then adult,
mysteries we unravel
to one another
makes welcome what carries
in our unpredicted arrival
to Mark, Janet
and their children.

'I work with Kate
in Toronto, in Canada,'
as we drink coffee
in the garden,
take a picture, overlooking
Dorset hills.

*

Up the curve of the street
into the Lion's Head, Sunday evening
of this pub.
up the curve of the street
into the singing which crosses us
to often bind strangers
for seconds together.
his pleasant, quiet face
 (from San Francisco, we learn)
yet here that release
to sing loudly with his friends,
and pint after pint of ale.
his friend, drunk, takes us in arm
with his tune, his sloppy kisses to Ros,
wet and we too pushed to join in
our slow letting go that grows
out from surprise, and talk as loudly
reach out of ourselves, caught
suddenly in their world. and to
then refuse his invitation
back to drinks at his home,
excusing ourselves
into Dorset dark.

   Long hollow sounds,
our heels in the moon:
we walk alone
our coughed *'en-dyo,'* that Japanese
'no thanks' too often, now sounding
as firmly in Ros, her Caucasian heart.
this we own too much to selves, a reticence
a privacy floating always, unseen
in air our palms close 'tween us,

the glimmering pact
up the corner
of Sherborne, our heels
flamed with the moon,
this sweet deserted night.

and turning up
the street retraced, past same
shop windows brightly lit, still
the eve for passersby, and we
are caught with fraught of bitter
-sweet tongue
our heads in reflection
of a Sunday's done:
Sunday morning

at Kitchie House to
get on the road.
Mark drives us to Dorchester,
a Sunday tour through Dorset, showing us
this Hardy land — Maiden Castle, traces of Roman
conquests, defeats left behind, for
archaeology to define.
Sunday morning at Dorchester in midst
of warm, grateful farewell,
his car's trunk gets jammed,
our packs tucked within.

such smile straining
at the edge where sharp nerves quaver that
burning with chance, towards
flash fire: wanting
to go, our delay,
his wanting to go,
his delay, knowing one another
as strangers too much now,
a visit throbbing excessively pro-
longed. at last standing here,
three of us, a garage we find open
and under grey skies the mechanic
breaks the lock free.

Ros offers Mark some money.
'He took it without hesitation,' she'd remark
afterwards.

Sunday afternoon, waiting how long?
the steady stream of cars, slowly,
'Sunday drivers' and nobody stops.
more waiting. pub lunch. more
waiting until tea.
we sit cream tea, across
from each other,
the languish when delicate nerves
burn to white stillness, of reminder
of heart's desire, filling with sweet cream, biscuits
and jam, the wordless minutes
of deepening gaze. 'This
is the last time I hitch-hike. Hitching
is friggin' shitty in Britain,'

words tossed out nearly every
half-hour, so always faster
than emotion, that swing
of my fist.

'Only if you believe,' she says
'Only if you believe,' again, while
jamming a scone

and driving in at last, the good
conversation with a stranger, this driver,
Sherborne is glorious
through the windshield, Sherborne
coming closer into view.
Damn! Damn

we go from one door to another,
bed and breakfasts so expensive here:
dismal edge to adventure,
that 'spirit of adventure' is
picking up plane
tickets FINALLY back in Toronto and

Sunday afternoon: Dorset Tourist Office closed.

To pay more than you want
for a room, the budget's blown.
to at last set down the bags,
have the hot steamy water and soap
on forehead and over closed eyes. to
walk at last, with knowing the night's bed,

be it expensive, and discover the narrow
hidden streets which become one's ventureful map;
such location and cool night,
and across the lawn to the cathedral,
we are taken by the echoes of organ, evensong
which transfixes and transforms
into the release from tired travel.
Sunday evening, few places open
to eat

we discover a Chinese take-away
and a street-bench to sit down;
and this counter-girl, a cook's daughter,
like family-run places
back home in Toronto; my heart
is discreet, into
its quick flutter, its quick
sublime dew, this lovely Oriental
with English accent, this change,
this signature of exotic
adjective to face
Oriental like mine, it's
what I am
to define, this want to become
Asian again as a-joining, edged
with that sweet change of pence
in her English palm.

Sunday evening, it was
desire and then, went into
Lion's Head, remember? I am
asking: don't want to leave —
       the travel, the shop windows, drunken talk,
       was from 'Frisco and pub-singing, regret

our shoes, with each
brilliant moonlit step, turning
out the light,
the traces of this night.

Sunday.
Monday morning, click.
got Ros' picture and
look, her right foot,
o well,
she's standing straight, but
look, right foot turned
over on its side —
her weight pushing down that way,
click. 'Heh!' she'll respond
later, the picture we develop.

Monday morning out of Sherborne
and Dorset, and bus, click again, the key and
chain affixed to plastic,
says, The Sherborne Inn,
click, which we mistakenly take away.
to carry along a place, we will
put it in a kitchen drawer months
later back home,

The Sherborne Inn it will say,
and do I ever hitch-hike again?
it's the bus at this coach stop,
where we'll leave Sherborne
behind.

*** and too there were

The Three Wishes

,

:

Coffees.
Luncheons.
Cream Teas.

bicycle leaning
on glass out front of
The Three Wishes
man pushing a cart,
 just walking by,
he is
door opening, the ing

a decent photograph,
again, we'll later
develop.

*

BATH

Into tepid waters
of unknowing,
the historic realm
: travel touches these
words, so sharply
defined by instance
the shapely events
of speech. here,
Caesar's footsteps
pressed upon
the back, this arch
of foot, of
conquering tongue
prescribes the way
of visiting,
and so,
 judging / the grammar
of the road.

THE DREAM OF BATH

this story, a history:
'The outstanding
memento or
    present.'

A TRAVELLER'S GUIDE TO BATH

(FOUND)

selling exciting coloured textile pictures and designs.
the home of the hamburger.
real Nottingham lace, luxurious big bath towels.
the myriad sidestreets and delightful backwaters.
in rather pleasant surroundings.
in Abbey Churchyard.
Purcell, Blow and Croft £1.50.
this month in Bath.
the gentle incline of gravel walk takes one past neatly
trimmed borders, precise flower gardens and eventually
Royal Crescent in its splendour.
dance the night away.
Abbey Churchyard.
various.
Roman remains in Britain.
moonboots, wellingtons, in fact, everything.
tea tasters coffee roasters.
prawn risotto, well-dressed salad.
flowers in Monmouth Street.
The Maharajah tandoori.
Broad Street, Westgate Street, Argyle Street,
Belvedere Lansdown Road.
minty, buttered new potatoes George Street.
Lord Nelson drank here, Courage Ales.
Henry's, Nero's Moles Club.
Abbey Churchyard.
bike hire.
Bristol Road, Wells Road, Oldfield Road, Bridge Street,
Pultney Weir, A46, A4, M4, M5, 63451, 28331, 92298531,
61111, 64446, 63075, 25481, 60655, 63333, 62831.

BATH FRAGMENT

tors

      or

stone.

piled forget,

circle   stones

      wind

or
bench, of slate
coverlet of primrose: meditation
or rest for the moment

                columns.

perimeter of deep
forgets,) Roman
pools.
        town called
) Bath.

*&

      or Pultney
   Weir and Bridge, Royal
  Crescent to The Circus, names, map
of Georgian-built homes

    The Circus
of stone, circles where
I pile, or eynter
her cervyx,
a certain rhapsody
Purcell, entering here,
there, the circle
(c)xommands, pulls
inherent, in her descendance
land of forgets, land left-be
-hind by her mother,
father after war,

    immigrant stones 3 stones
    move. gently, she knows gently
    she does;
calls England
her pelvic ridge.

NEW SONG
for Thomas, Laurie & Tamsin Clark

THE COTSWOLDS

juice for the tamsin
quiche for the thomas
new potatoes for the laurie
fresh mint for the rosalind
garden squash for the gerry.
all appointed. slicing and pouring.
a little walk upon
rockness hill. a verse
for the garden
we stir, summery breeze
to remember
a sheaf of fine leaves.

TASTING NOTES: ROCKNESS HILL

Cutting the home-baked quiche,
ladling courgettes, new potatoes
we appoint all: some for each: à table
together, overlooking the soft valley.
taste of village sprite, country
walk the railed footpath before dinner
we appoint
all for the childhood:

  sleep which will come gently
to Tamsin-girl. dreaming,
there is cutting,
ladling the last cling
of sweet melted butter and
the walking
we name such day,
this close of day;
the fragments dust
beneath our nails, we address
our families, our good friends, quick
disappearing sun chipping
off the bright cottage walls.

HOLIDAY IN EUROPE: IN RETROSPECT

TORONTO — SEPTEMBER 1982

1. Espresso

Language which haunts
the streets

    white marks,
      broken line
    on pavement —

  cigarette butts.
          and other sewage

rain trickles,
enters
seams which,

 inviting the voice,
quench humid.

2. Souvenir

Night's antica houses
passageways through
hot-flowers
past the palpable
sleep of this
black dog or that
blonde
/ashen heavy steps,
stones, dusty windows
scrape
to polish oracular,
love, once passed
present through sentient
climbing,
rhododendrons, cars'
grammatic traffic
: relation, meeting.

 transients,
each country, postage
visits, marks on each other,
trying compassion
and holding each embrace
as spelled, the baggage
failed. in
        translence.

3. Espresso 2

Now returned, city of warm
humid rains, this a
home where language
haunts with excess
coinage, cliché, archetype.
think, therefore
we know not: heh! a bad joke, expensive
cliché, archetype. we are;
here are the chill tongues with drab verbs,
which incise their acts in a thirsty
uneventful night. night's café,
with lights,
yes, espresso again.
because of its dark: wet silence
upon winter's parch,
 hitting this brain re-
calling streets where
moon invades with open-eyed
sleep, somnolent pearl
with sharpened figures,
one too clearly sees,
which we think, automatically
frees.

BOOK III

AQUEDUCT

(1984-87)

PARIS

OPEN PALM, FIRST MEMENTO

RUE GAY-LUSSAC

1.

Under the open shutters,
the eaves,

autumn so particular
a voice, and such leaves

marguerites, white freesias
and bright scarlet oeillets —
stacked in market stalls,
or such cuts of beef
and veal, the cheese and leeks
cardoons, plums all
which try the mouth;

it is a speech I know it
silent excited

all the body pays for, attends
with it, quietly here
to this window, calls
the stalls we descend
rue Mouffetard.

2.

To feel such streets, place and this
the right slant,
angle   askew
an answer that departs
these lips, try the reason, a maquette, such
hisses trans/action: light shivers
on a string
            /light cream.
It is done,
that way it's like that.
In the hands on cool clay even that
way the mouth pours out
the streets in Paris pull
in.

3.

When you think it flies

a bird.

Eggs on the plate

egg on your
face.

4.

Damn it's the noise it's when people   speech, speech / lunch can cut with a knife so deep in the day's light deep of working, of lunch of forks, of butter melting, sliding into the pan quick forks three eggs stirred together balance on the time the schedule of carnet, the appointments of writing down the little explosions in the spine. All the time.

5.

It is all done
Ros, dear,
the streets and cafés of visits
we did, all done fallen, the tinge
of chestnut leaves
the autumn's the catch of regard
those iron balconies eyed
from low.

So walking. And I am sitting
watching, the words that place
     /you again
here/   uh there
all round   the moves
in me, an auricle mumble
outside this pump that surge
where you ever
hesitate me
awake.

6.

Softly all, mesdames
messieurs softly all the rolls to m'sieur'dame
the fruits in markets, grey snails or large
Burgundys its specific regards which garnish
our platters, our hopes.
The whims of voice. Voice his and hers'ieur/dame
the masculin/feminin
'Love Me Tender' an Elvis,
like lover's   lovers' talk
directly and delicately taste particular-
ly sweet, a precise cuisine of say
fifties the decade's culture again branché[11] in this city's
light, the vocables upon vocables
in market streets
are sold (they have) by
the gram.

THE TABAC: IT IS FOR HER

Driven into the energy, the wave
of music — of chansons, of
packets of cigarettes piled high, strike time,
the fluorescent lights in Tabac des Écoles; her
hands wet washing dishes, a woman's hands,
wet, juice of lemons, this sharp
in chansons, this express I sip. Hands at rest
against this copper-tin bar feeling
more by sight, as if described by this light
which decodes. All this. As this, way feet
ache on the floor which I care less to describe,
such two planted and too much
walking turning silence upon into words
that rush to romance a delicious
ache so Gallic. Too much the invasion
when notes streaming out of this radio
every chord proper, leaves me this Tabac
and the property of phrases in excess
and knot place to hide.

But still, still, drink, then drink some more,
together with seconds, her look, she's wiping,
'Bonne nuit, madame,'
'Bonne nuit, monsieur,'
hunger for the moon, that moon outside (a St. Michel bus
for Port d'Orléans).
That light — with no time or place
for silence, I could explain;
yet though with each step
'bout its perimeter I walk,
there is shadow and silent wax
holding all numbers, all desires
in just place.

THE KITCHEN

O that clap and clatter of metal pots
and pans, the kitchen odours
soft: celery and carrots softening in butter,
veal bones browning, mustard and cream,
buckwheat or perhaps simply,
a colander of chervil and snipped laurel,
the dried lavender and anemone. Open doors
swollen with damp, the thinning rain.

                Objects
have their singular mute power and relentless, assign
/strongly take their
loot of passion, each turn of the head,
watchfulness. Substances
and concepts arrive not un-
engaged; such to
forget or regret

each date
an object infinite
as long as it's felt,
  an evening, a nightbed tumbled
together,

that ringing of pans.

MAGHREBINS

Such uneasy thing. To hold
weight unchosen and
attend to it. It is this, la chose
qui t'attend. Uneasy,
hostile, not comfortable with un-

easily, it.
Arched back,
turn that other cheek,   *toi*, to
turn that other cheek,   and
one's back for support
and wait.

'But they do not leave, plan to destroy our names
populate even our purest breath,

                        (here is LePen[12])
       writing history,
    to describe what pain
is this country mine, my God,   the heathens,
who refuse to become as us to taste as that speech
a mass with organ serves

us all, the madeleines sweet, *la chose qui m'attend*

this weight of troubled speech, my hostile
body, such
 instrument to bear it.'

Paris, a city   divide
city of foreign tongues crowd
of dark, haired, unchosen speech,
seated in every Métro car

       cette chose de la langue, to parse
the *lourd* of *parole.*

WHO FIDGETS

Smock:

Hard leather heels, in running, arms are held waist high, back upright, as is the perfect form for jogging. She is dressed in a pale blue cotton smock, a firm but relaxed figure, descending down the street.

Up above, she — or another is reaching beyond the black iron balcony a pale blue sky, and s' almost hollow the sound of the heels, arms moving adeptly to her run, descent. It is tender, it is soft a movement that alights from such falling, caresses across his tongue. The tastes, he pauses, and wet, he guesses now at this (agreement) what point tenderness problematically penetrates to speech, that space which, a thickness, the heart which trickles its notion of faith, when the terrible motion she returns when the movement that caress, fi—, that now the fists loosely clenched, when the hard leather heels stop, when the blue smock billows upwards as she hesitates an ascent (and the water presses forth, rims his mouth a second time, it has, this overflowing river, happened before, when he looks behind).

Marble:

The memory it takes from his mouth. The way day begins, the café. The way every day begins with the emptied plastic ashtrays and the circle: a mouth filled too strongly with cloud, which each day problematically opens, yet wants instead its till of open and crisp blue sky (reminding perhaps in a sense of starched crinoline, its clear brittle voice) and yet that temper of colours which vigorously move across the quarters over the chrome-edged traffic, over the everpresent river nearby. There is too much noise, just too much and it fills every small packet, package which one covets in hope, for secrets. And such touch. The touch too vigorous, too anxious, too bold. A waiter too rude, too quick, coins slapped on the table (the noise) a bold sauce full of beef in the mouth — and yet, the humour (a climate) wants more.

He remembers the heels, not by click of stitched leather wedged on pavement nor glissant marble — brittle concentration; but the conversation and the pelvic, which slid past him glissant marble or like pale fuchsia perfume. Polished marble, refracted light from a window. Pillars, winding staircases. Figures moving juxtaposing one another. Fascinated not by paintings, by art, by the steady light of an outstretched Madonna's wrist, but the sight of flesh of a woman's rigid heel, her tendons prisoned upright, walking away.

The smock billows upwards, while papers and dust blur in the pale blue flight.

Every day begins with the emptied plastic ashtrays (promoting without fail some anisette drink) and the circle: the way wetness rims a cup, the dribbles down its sides, a hesitation, too loose a bottom lip. A fascination with the river has the fisherman who fishes there, a seine net, watching it all overflow.

When he glances behind, a cup barely to the lip, he sees the cyclist but only for a second, the bright marine blue of his nylon windgear, the muscles of his calf, the tendons extended upwards, body thrust forward, no face to the call (he sips another time), the chrome of the two wheels spinning, and it is gone.

Ornamental:

As he files his nails, the handles of a storage cupboard fall. The line of descent he listens, feels too in the tension of wrists, the fracture of a middle finger once, in that pain, then an articulation of the emerald note etched onto the violet, the copper is this what she wears, wears dangling from her ears. Zinc too, the elbows rest upon, polishes the strain of how many coins slapped rapidly in a till, the reactive key of register, returned àlà to the zinc bar (a tip) how many still counting hours for so many coins which calculations of client and server co-invest, the labour of a treatise of poring through records, pouring out drinks, an affective economy, re agenda geometry. When the smock blows skywards, when he arranges the chessboard, in the colour of light, he is too arranged on the rue Jacob, the Sunday, of course, 'it is a gift,' so be it — they tell, 'that which is life.' A turn of the bare heel against the cool carbon pedestal leg of the round table, well then, but no, the billowing up, billowing up on the rue Jacob, standing outside the shop window, they are earrings, she inside, seated there, has crafted (looks briefly up at) has crafted them by hand, based on Navajo, Ivory Coast and III Empire Napoleonic design, and they lie flat as coins in this vitrine, they could hang, with the weight as insistent on the ears, the cool pink lobes of another, another equal, could be made just for that her.

Other:

When he glances behind, cup barely to the lip, he sees the cyclist, the bright sad narcissus, the bright marine blue of his nylon windgear, the muscles of his calf, the tendons extended upwards, body thrust forward, no face to the call (he sips another time), the chrome of the two wheels spinning.

THE BEND

    that,

    scream which comes
    (low hum)
    from deep within &
     erases all current news,
    affairs,
    ears perked to radio on
    your table.

Maybe you are preparing a dinner.

Météo:
         opens the wet doors
the sea wander smell violet
kelp
 on the beach; or at the fishmonger — a bed
for poaching lemon sole.

that,
for instance, that voice
of mumbling, but deep *words* from
the poor drunkard woman, her flaccid fur,
in the Métro, who smelled
of off-wine and vomitting.   That way,

what's the *météo*?
And (can we call it *dance*?)
she rose silent (pre-
meditation) to attack (choreo-
graph)

and pull violent this woman, too prim
accompanied by husband, en route
dressed in expensive black fur. Disdain,
and then to sit, now pressed
next to me, I imagine
this smell on my sleeve, a headline
flash, *Le Monde, Libération*, a stain.

(whose side are we on?) preparing dinner

which side of the sentence do we
implant ourselves with each slice
of shallots with each slice of cèpes,
with the stomach rumblings of hunger,
or the pitless waltz of fear,
key of deep music?

Le Monde, L'Équipe — for the sports,
this radio —
all current affairs, you see
that which music writes in
us to make speech clear, decided,
lyrical, articulate by gourmet

that, low hum.

TRANSIT

Ta-tá, ta-tá, ta-tá, ta-tá, ta holding,
hold; steady the clear fine light
hold it, this accordion echoes down the tiled corridors, music
footloose black shoes, holding accordion, his arching back supporting
such instrument, holds, peaks, the measure of a lasting bright.

No time now me in his bright, to hold to self the hostile this uneasy weight, thing of not knowing a home, a place to rest crumpled creased papers and notes, heavy table and pen. O, arching back, to collect the sous busking peaks.

The import is suchly delivered each day like mail, or affixed to used tickets, footprinted on the floors of Métro stations. Hold to the pattern which arrives, arrives unsignalled in the passing, smell of charcuterie chickens spit-roasted with garlic and thyme filling the head, and the sight of passing umbrellas, held soldierly against the rains.

TWILIGHT TIME
> *for James Deahl and Gilda Mekler*

The switchblade of life which is
not to speak of danger, of threat

the test corporeal. But quick
utterance, eyes

too blood-bearing weight and tone, dried
the several years' metal.

Here is this juke-box,
the song is *Twilight Time* (Platters, c. 1959)
sung now translated to French, sharpens
such place giving the bread

and these tables   arborite, and
plastic ashtrays, promoting some anisette drink.
Coat-stands, empty; dismal curtains,
embroidered giving
onto wet dusk streets, the trains near south,
 by St. Lazare.

A waiter and patron talk chomage, unemployment
in France, world revolving
always the quick same music, let us translate
no job such noise. A melody's imply,
a music overdubbing bears the metal with its taste
of cuts, its forged lottery ardour.

This is a switchblade. It. Like the hail, by chance, fate.
Switchblade, it holds me
does at the neck, is a danger, is a threat,
boring, is complacent and oo,
I forget
my body.

       'J'ai faim. Mon chien a faim.
       S'il vous plait' the sign reads

Twilight Time, a music: simple breathing
for this and other meals in cafés.
But those others, who has the money
for that music from the chef's stove,
the mouth repeatedly craves?

NOTES ON FORM: THE LOUVRE

1a)

That writing you wear
across your body,

                    template, pure marble
          and muscular pose; and secret

your tongue.

And then, the dream across your feet.

In the hot sands, we look, paths stretching
out beyond Port Lligat;
how swollen tongues feel now, attendant
with the mollusc,

as on bed, as shell, and curled
and feet upon high,
will sleep arrive?

b)

The markets of ripe produce seem so distant now as we take coffee standing
amidst cigarette ashes, sawdust at the bar: the cheese, the artichoke, the
sardine — all these out there, not within, unheard and so, here we are
concentration we are relax, we are familiar glasses and money, our feet.

These ways dreams are scored on body and
body's event,

'all'

it is frozen, here, here
a carved marble form, a *switch*   Breathing
at last cool air, we

the open window in August,
voile curtains fluttering,
        moonlit,

   a deep night.

2

I have stepped here before, half
hieroglyph   and half night,
or then at least such memory, an ancient language, a time.

This 'tired head' casque now, tired
is half exposed by crack in the idea
of casque. The full; the empty, some fractured
clay line, for all to see

   half hieroglyph and half
   colour: emotion, a grief connotation
   for instance, at a loved one's
   death, or paralytic distress over
   starving dark children in the report
   of news; the colour of speech;[13] in action

        the hieroglyph once carved
        of little birds, the message, implements
        foodstuffs and directives like slogans
        on T-shirts, patch the self,
        self's event
        and there are knots to
constantly untie,

with stiff hands. pick a-'
part
that moonlit dark.

3

... and to say she was walking
she knew it she was

that way, the pointed finger of her

  figure, so stilled even if
  she was walking,

or to say she
was sitting, sitting
then, it was also

that still, the way
crowds moved about her watching,

the way the planets
revolved without cease
that way the moon

shared its round
light

and illumined, mirrored
her blue breast, the circle of returning
sleep.

3a)

With hands or stars which cross beyond intimate perimeter
her breasts are tenderly covered;

and yet are the charmed, inscribed
as tablets, recount of birth and battle,

part of the necklace the shape
seers want magic for
the dictations of what will pass
beneath the lintels

we will underline
in our annals

in our wills
we had underlined.

4

Without light. Without
real light. A dark corner
of late afternoon,

    laid not on display,
    under glass though:

    rock, smooth carved wood or even
                            netting,

(or if,   time
when one was about
to speak)

and also
those small sticks especially,
the way thread joined them at their tops, over small, exact
distance.

word   —   word   —

(that feeling catch,
in the mouth, eh?) join
    shimmering in speech created

such sewn,
        /that past
      so now
        repeated,

        =light, it dazzles
          the string.

4a)

Television:

With such, his death, the arrival of the most sumptuous feast he could have imagined when he jokingly had said, 'For my last supper, I'd like ...' and such did arrive the birds, the tools of the trade, the postage stamps should he want to send postcards, the athletic wear, even a cargo ship was inscribed to the famous death, prescribed previously by the physician, all in the cardboard box which said *This Side Up* the volume was very loud, the images remained, people were watching, they had guidebooks with clear indication of recommended viewing.

5 (Wardrobe of Self)

What were you wearing on your head?
Was it green? Was it metal?
Wa
    s it necessary?

5a)

To be standing, to be sitting.
To be moving, to be kneeling.
To be standing there
to be kneeling to be walking there.
To be standing to be kneeling
to pick apart,
to be standing, to be kneeling;
to pick a-
part that
moonlit dark.

5b)

Upon the head, a cat is a luxurious rest indeed,
ornament you wear for its look

it cast in marble, blue quartz or clay
carved on a fibrous yes, a tenuous descent
the head such casque
rolling as bobbin does.
It comes apart alas, moonlit a beaded necklace (let's gather up
the milky drops shall we? And follow the path) it
is walking

 away.

6

To hold and to point
to lay down

action.

    Riding
   the back
    of donkey, your own
    hand

Sway,

from hand to hand
holding back emotion, up
there. Life, you see it, point

standing there (firm), letting war
         happen,
again.

                    (I hold and point
                    out, I lay) there

6a)

(an afterword)

If these words mean but
         /endeavour to change,
lean these forward,
that feel it, head, who you
are, in the hands the one
transforming, making
the world as if

wheat   barley   marble   flax   lichen   lizard

basalt   onyx   apple

* HEAD-CARRIER'S ANNOUNCEMENT *

*Headless, and a case artisan-made
to carry the head in. Containment,
a strategy of war by man is
a has-been he, remains
(to be seen when one digs for)
under this ever, to look under
parched earth or bedded on in
burial-cloths: lift it open
(passing garden, lemon perfume)
the seeds within, same the seeds
in clay hand-made by turn or
shaped into uh, jug — the Greeks'
amphora there's a spread of smile,
to get into (the vale of tears) it's
the crack of the found, container
by archaeology*

*Carry the sentences too
in this case:
for the head that for the dead is
what I here announce   come carrying
the head and I
present this head to you
for your very own collection. Of
capital importance, editorially,
it bears
a column's
worth of weight.*

* HEAD — CARRIER'S ANNOUNCEMENT *

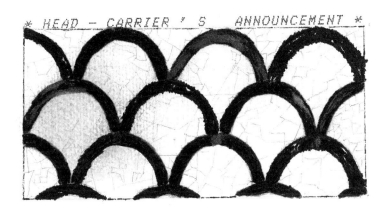

Headless, and a case artisan-made
to carry the head in. Containment,
a strategy of war by man is
a has-been he, remains
(to be seen when one digs for)
under this ever, to look under
parched earth or bedded on in
burial-cloths: lift it open
(passing garden, lemon perfume)
the seeds within, same the seeds
in clay hand-made by turn or
shaped into uh, jug - the Greeks'
amphora there's a spread of smile,
to get into (the vale of tears) it's
the crack of the found, container
by archaeology.

Carry the sentences too
in this case:
for the head that for the dead is
what I here announce   come carrying
the head and I
present this head to you
for your very own collection. Of
capital importance, editorially,
it bears a column's
worth of weight.

NOTES ON WRITING AND MEALS

The everyday type of writing and everyday meals continue the line longer, break each rule cooked breathing of breath, taste the perfume, breathe to carry it further into the nostrils and at the stove or table sniff, or the loss — sustenance that happened you see, on the boulevard St. Germain or avenue Bosquet — or never part of the planetree leaves that fall with each autumn. Breathe do I the plain breathing is as plane leaves fall, that autumn in these lungs and every day, every day we are at pots and pans and scrubbing away. Such talking away such meals say Chez Germaine talk and order push the line, with now lower lip ready muscatorily defined with that anticipatory, that habit of ready, to try to speak to a community, every day.

BOY

          or what is the subject
            of the conversation
          outside,   or the kitchen.   (he

           Through the hall,
hears)   you can't concentrate
          on the boy's gaze
          fixed attention to your
            object.

                                            (the

adverb)

A PARIS MUSEUM

We no longer think upon or celebrate with the climb which calls the ladder from the heart, like the free-willed touch, donated. Picture: to lie prostrate in bed, a ladder stretches magically from the barren, even battered chest.

Or too, there's the robe to dress the canker by a probe with the tick-tock watch or meter going, it's the geometric phrase in patter(n) in death so cubist
   that parole arrives before we can regain the ornate take of gilded thought, past plundered.

1

a)

No longer, or at least
thought negligent, celebration
wow ladders from one's heart,
neat giving heat rises by touch.

b)

As firemen's ladders lead upwards
from the heart or, snakes — the boardgame of coming down, what a sight.
No longer actually do we climb
that way, like charmed youthful expeditions to Nepal, thought
   or to celebrate; that
giving rise by touch clitoris or penis on bed
or the train's cargo of indecisive, *hmm*   *good insurance policy*,
strain contact each other's physical needs.

e.g. Picture: ladder leading up into the clouds.
　　　Beyond these clouds, to the *Receiver's* outstretched
　　　arms, as per usual, background painted lovely blueness:[14]
　　　concentrated hands, like cerveux au beurre noir — a bit odd,

　　　delicate, but sweet — good hand-eye coordination,
　　　gentle palms, heavenly touch.

2 (the forget)

Strong design
or feign
　　　of hand
slight
gesture. Tool
 of weave   lapis
lazuli, ochre.
The cobalt without doubt
　　night /
　　　　　day

　allures.

3

Allure is a tongue
the way the ear
dressed,
 comes seductive speech, missing
the object,
　　　desire.

4

Fish, flapping in bowl

  so dry.

Or shrimp, tiny guys
grey still,   you are

feeling   then

in hand,
  that flicker

    at instance,
(thought) of stove, (life but instant)

         insists
      the fiery pan, with tight-fitting lid
readied with oil.

(regain)

SHE: TO BEGIN WITH CONJUNCTION (END AS SUNG)

to begin with conjunction,
I do not know the speech. I do not know.

The blue permitting glass high is cast,
light in yet its dark vault
which holds a numen hesitant

movement, project music
borne in hands, breath   what next?

Look, these hands of mine, holding
pen,
  or shimmer floating,
         midday

 sun in river. There could be

a bridge come upon, bridge / which crosses that
where tempi and tune joins
with light, hands unbound yet, that constant gravity: here,

organ pipes reach up
the blue depths of intensity

of her rose window, and
red, yellow

of her rose window, and
red, yellow,

look, could be
beginning,
a bridge, the force come upon
in hands, a light
enhancing gravity.

PROVOKE

: 4TH ARRONDISSEMENT; 9TH ARRONDISSEMENT; 15TH ARRONDISSEMENT
PARIS — OCTOBER 1984; MAY 1987

1. work, speech

O, that desertion one holds in the end of everyday speech, how with each
comma we take in breath, that next vehicle, that which a lover whispers by
the ear, a phrase, a descriptive pattern in a private language, in such conspiracy, complicity we cannot rest with the ordinary goods we own.
When the wind blows up the tunnel and the next train arrives, its capacity of
strangers standing speechless hip to hip, the smell of sulphur lingers, and the
interminable common freight: one book, one newspaper, one dialogue
between friends, all arrives with the framed finality of cinema, sure as a
platform of trains, but mute and chaplin in ultimate degree.

2. architecture, media

He is holding by the hair, thin strands, that which is between, the depart, the
fixture, the pain if pulled, or the angle turned in a window when eyes meet
it.   3rd storey on the right — through the front door, the small screen of a
television through an opened window. Holding by the hair, such pulled, it too is
pleasure; and on the screen — bright orange backdrop set   for cooked green vegetal
soup in its tureen, just this flash and gone.

A detergent smell, lemon and chlorine caught ah, chance without name,
damp clothes hung on rails in the courtyard, filled with garbage bins. When
he returns to the street from the dark court's recess, the avenue filled with a
shapeless autumn sunlight, and the hair which holds him transparent here
could break into a silence, those moments prized deeply in a noisy Sunday,
market-way café, they fall after the bite of dry salt pork sausage.

*

O so kiss yes, she, that give and ah so what once, the quarrels then come; how then strange yes then apart when she, s, that note again, that, not once you were not, here.

Having been here once before in reading books having   burdened been here standing before transient crowd Gare St. Lazare this crossways of moving pigeons in this litter-strewn plaza, having passed don't we always with baggage. Thus here rests the desire of the tongue to taste what letters bring with their perfume of glue, their spectacles of words, their silence, in alphabet of gestures, of having been here once before in the sharp Saturday sun.

3. a recapture

The lottery tickets fly in sale, they do, they do fly with holiday's target. Leave and arrive. A salad a table, Auvergnat[15] ham and firm-rind cheese on soft bibb lettuce. A bottle of water to top a tumbler of some green mint syrup. Casanis anisette on ice. What call you silence but the missed numbers of a sharp gamble, a swing under trees, or a chair left vacant by blunt departure.

4. spare time

One's seated on the briliant blue moulded seat, awaiting the predicted train. One decides, one's decided; one decides, one's decided. A newspaper fact a second page blows to the platform edge, there walks he, the steps of desire. The edge, open the book of city maps, city plan. One's a decided smell odd. Smell of sulphur lingers. Smell of emmenthal lingers. Smell of café lingers. Smell of anis lingers. Smell of damp clothes lingers and the flash of a lottery magic and gone. Arrive, arrive, arrive, arrive, arrive, arrive, arrive, arrive, arrive, arrive, arrive, arrive.

PALE: A CUISINE

This pale, robin's-egg blue cup and saucer; that thinness — colours so much draw the lines of existence, insisting their way to the frontiers: what be distinguished; what be not. Then, life begins, each movement; that before we can destroy the body's lean to the present, there is this harmony of body to colour, to the composition before us.

Sometimes so difficult in the presence of words, signs, to (take place), to let eventuality process to eventuality with inertia — for every gesture of language — *Fast Dry Cleaning Pressing, Cigarettes,* the Hotel signs swinging in the light — there is aperture, the dream of the first word as it deposits into the field: 'Love, speak to me,' fresh-cut roses delivered to the door — 'It was a wonderful evening' it says, 'Just a little something' it says, 'Roses for a Miss-So-and-so,' says the young rough-skinned man in blue jeans and sneakers — and the van, marked with dirt and bits of corrosion around the wheels, pulls away.

This robin's-egg blue cup, so pale; sunlight streams a diagonal across the page you are reading, knife slicing sandwich, 'Egg salad on white, please,' thinness,

delicate and blue; delicate, I remember that spray of flowers on the white bone china, not roses mind you, nor real flowers, but the decor of a meal, set down and once tasted, the body's grasp of that lean, in quiet passion, quiet reverie.

THE GOING FOR A WALK AROUND

Start:

Smell, vigour, the mo-
ment well, it ripens,
melons held
dropped seconds

(after)
ripened
a long way,
home.

Rain: (an opening

It's not / it's true
the fresh rain
a shower, a storm
 making unnecessary
                            the way
any kind of question
? any sort of demand   (is lost

        an opening)

\>

Distance:

Is more about word than otherwise
about more taste and about
speed
the way images boom: *L'Express* weekly, blousons,
Gitanes, Agnès B, Alain Delon. Cross here, there:
cross each 'T' the line of how   (he with 'T' makes The, here with 'T'
                                            makes There)
do we exist in a place.

Located by quick, by pitch by the quick
formal words graces' happenstance
like here, 'Sir,'   kiosk where   'at least, at least
I've got a job,' that feeling, with maps,
postcards to define the territories be-
tween the days   and the loss of
     where. 4 cards, '8   francs   please.'
Thank you,   sir. 'Thank   *you*, sir. Good   bye.'
Bye.

   Where (keys).   Where (me).
Scarf around the neck around
every around all, all very French. This kiosk, this place,
postcard notates upon delivery to address, that Delon:

  where
cross the 'T'   angles, streets
cross and radiate in
all directions of quick,
traffic circles the wherewhere
where.
Where where.

TEXTE

Or then, how to temper that flash, that skin, the delicate pale blue dayblooms which transmit light, for which we have no exact ways to part lips and hold pattern. The hold sensuous in the mornings, finds the break — in grey clearing past rain — the workers taking muscadet or kir in small glasses at the bar, after loading cleaned carcasses destined for restaurants and brasseries. A flash, which marks us suddenly blemished or goose-pimpled flesh, words raised from the page, against the truant and habit smell of frites or dripping cut meats for Tunisian sandwiches, such harbingers dispatched to persuade against good judgment and taste, for which the night had prepared us, ushered with black ties and white cotton gloves. Crowds gather at the bar, hands upon hip. O, the coins, change set upon dish, elbows polish tin, such porcelain too. We proceed. We place our tongues against our nearest sores as braille, we step gingerly, ascendant and marked, towards words which point to the future — seated against the drying streams of urine on pocked pavement, trailing from the corners of shadowy buildings we pass they touch us secretly, moving past splintered wooden crates stained with residues of fruits, the finest bibb lettuce even, browning, once verdant as the speech we now ourselves try to form, preparing at last, to hold as new lovers, our strong strangers, they beckon from oncoming nights.

LE TEMPS

Postponed to later, to then apprehend
the letter for a latter
time, seed, sent by mail, to
comprehend, ahead
what we now know
to know it's not
the forgetting, and to pick
up the place, newfound
again.

CONTEXTE

The mix of pleasure, *The Pleasure of the Text* set in the mode of held glasses of muscadet at the bar, taken by patrons, set in the words of pleasure in the reading, right the way ideas set and then space in the voices arranged, and the smell of cigarettes. The way — the painted tiles of 1900 Les Halles, tin metal bar called Le Plat du Jour and the frosted rose lamps produce all that my body can bear of pleasure, let us admit, of then sending by telegraph a thought to you friend, of suggesting that you read this book in another place, with another setting, with other hands.

L'ÉGLISE DE LA MADELEINE
for John Goss

Does one want invention? Does one want this glove? Or moving sent. That music which twines so in repeat, fugue as it brims fugue as in race returned to this air, the nostrils ready ready, the chords of light, thread, thread they bang at this stable door. Heart wrought by loud pantheon, organ untethered now as in past, the seeds sown with chords, this wilderness of wild gentle animals, harp even by vestige of architecture so bright, built on what's dark, what one craves to know in thine next verse. With such hands in key, to North; the pine; and pickerel caught in filament tune as one's too gripped in St. Martin's or Christchurch, their bell-hewn clues to matins verse. O, to be taken not by mouth, rumour, of wherein lies power — birth, death, but music as it strains and leans forward, candles brightly aglow, template of pulse, temperature flush at once on hands which scale carved stone walls to skies, to high-pitched air or throaty bells, to dig with force the earth's loam in spring, the damp soil-headed leaves of autumn, to make with hands the music one arches, oh, the colour, indeed gold leaf, that rich harmony. Tell me, where palms upturned might go, to form a cushion for seating or kneel, to tap at shoulders of suffering ones, 'lightly,' to pray else in the organ pipes where ducts well full, fingers moving blood-let across bell-boards know, the pedals' push damn. Want heat in winter. That fast, that prayer, that dance any but; more. Let all but; let all be mad sentence; pray; kneel. O, kindly.

FRIENDLY MESSAGE

(L'ÉGLISE DE LA MADELEINE)

O, lung-eaten breath be that stream
be that stream of bread with wine; for they,
yet comes now stomach's cancer, our own
monsters grey weapons to kill kill each with nuclear
force. O, lung, where harvest music, the pipe's
aching breath. Let taste let pass through, does
carry majesty look,
sweet diet and kiss then tumour, tumour again, and
then
dance, for this way to transform/malignant
fear, and play joyous the woodlot and brook,
as O dream this is I know, but
honest, I am your friend, decay to next simple
breath, this speech is coming in generous life's
name

TRIO
for (Sir) Robert Filiou(sous)[16]

a. Bruise

Dark is red the way your bruise is, you think, you're along the stream of blood. (and
then, a bit out of circulation, the traffic's fierce red,
take your very red pencil and mark a dot on this bruised finger, as if
a pin-prick. SOLUTION? you lean with increasing age, flowering towards the dark, which you realize is a shell, a scallop) the red fruit.

b. Oysters: a brasserie remedy (for the Common Heat)

Take the best, a tightly closed shell, barely moves even if forced,
cold, alive.

... cut that raw, runny graystone in half. Care not to cut oneself.
Raise the empty half-shell to the centre of your forehead and leave it there, abandoned. 'Nuclear power?' someone once asked. No thanks.

c. American in Paris (doesn't fit)

In this sentimental, 'mon dieu' Paris
rain, she exits the taxi, Mickey Mouse
in her arms.

April, an inch of perfume,

   god, she's priddy, must be —

my oyster!

p-r-i-d-d-y, to be correct, is p-r-e-t-t-y

all the same that sentimental.
Where do I stop? Is this now a well-made poem?
A badly made? A poem at all?
and in her arms, back to Mickey,
... back to 'Manhattan' eau de cologne concentré.

THE PAINTED GARDEN

They are then, those gestures behind doors, the balance of colour and form (force) of such scale, when the light discreetly shines what imagination paints. The shallots or peaches, the rippled cloth tumbling out of its basket, that taste of cracked walnuts. When we enter, there are chairs in the corner of our view, a napkin has been placed, and with, an Oriental print waxed with dirt (beneath our fingernails).

The difficulty in capturing the exact tone of pain at the moment of entry, for just at such point when tossed in the night while asleep there was this dolorous wounded voice. Soft. Soft tension of magenta pressed into powder, the flesh of the hand. To walk off the boundaries in this field of night, counting, to turn with preposition, as splinter, guided by penetrating form, chairs in the corners even closer in our view, into the new subject, the outstretched perspective's thumb, the table leg, the knife, the nutcracker, unrelenting in their painted pattern.

When she holds up her fan, the light is cast out — a kind of undressing (dictionary on the table, a knife to cut, the flesh of its blade) (the sound of an exotic leathered emotion) beneath the dark dress, eyes mount the words, the vocables surface: wet worms. And the cool moon. Enter this night with a stare.

I can remember then, the precision of that meal, when the proprietor had ushered me to the corner, the corner table, and I ate by candlelight, the wax dripping off-line, onto the cotton cloth. Eggs, hot, yet still liquid and yellow in their sweet warm cream, the tureen to fingers was hot, I would taste and inhale the odours into me. And the crisp, almost smoke salt skin of a duck confit in its soft giving sauce, a tableau of puréed carrots fanned with ridges, and those sweet white potatoes, still vegetable crisp, speaking of their presence in the earth.

DAY: AN ARCHITECTURE

Out and up from below,
the cold, white
frost hard under heel;

      out
and up into,
frozen day, brittle angle,
elbow, an iron fence cutting
a sound forming behind the lips:
air, open space
the architecture of
thought, those which same things
but the parlance in French
words, the some caught
semblance brush the ears, one understands
— as they say,
'the drift
of things.'

The drift of things, the slowly lengthening shadows
cast — the classic and formal;
six-storey buildings, tergal sheers on windows,
drapes tied back; and from there
sweeping views over the city and river,
the plan of things.

When she looks out
and down from above,
always the depart (the soft odours emerging
from the kitchen)
the mouths' suffix, afflection to
words, never ending this space the vision
not looking back with his ancient leather valise,
belt tying it together, the divide

it opens. Breathe, breathe, resuscitation.
That feeling which emerges from stomach, viewing out and
up from this café
and too, latches that taste it lingers
in the mouth.

TRANSLATION FROM THE FRENCH

when I didn't or did.

'It's not the grave.'
  (mortal   sin or non)

*

Tables, white so wrapped with
light. Attention of work, and sun
across / touch the cup,   coffee then.
Oh, tables wrapped   space
beyond edges, far,   here am I the
heart's movement, cased
in light. Oh, but it. Feeds miles,
its white surface, an enrapture
between here, and which or where,
ever. Asks.

PARIS

Shelter from rain or
this bite (tongue) cachet
of defiant syllable movement
(accidental) like that
quick trip (a bathroom)
shelter from rain or
another's harangue, by closing
the mouth,
opening the umbrella upside
down, catch the opposite
catheter conveniencer
of lessons learned day
by day, especially when
people say, 'Nice weather
we're having, eh?' Eh is
the way we bring life together
and catch the Canadian, glorious
sunset, and nap it with an intelligent
sauce, a healthy shrug
of the shoulders, say,
a shelter,
   the sunset still glowing
   across Lake Temagami.

ARROW: SKETCH OF LANDSCAPE

Here   (there)

on the hearth, this warm hearse
moment bright my eyes.

Two shimmering figures on the dark dust
two train tracks.

An arrow curves
in mouth from there;

and falling,
and taste
of this arrow in a speech
winding
direction across my tongue,

somehow, *the smell of paints,* and too
engravers factory the senses and
enamels but nowhere
but the hearse parked briefly
on the tongue. And then, on the curve
towards point,

train sounds
calling, approach
of day fills the,

my opened mouth 'Ah,'
the, night and feathered

and its two fi(n)gures,
its fading tracks.

'n'

*

It is always what's wanted, what's before the eyes and then like gifts, gone. The long hair so forceful, wild before the face, the black leather blouson, and the shiny black patent leather shoes, holding the bony, well-formed feet. That look she has, a profile as if harried and those lips neither pouting nor hidden, lips which hold seemingly for minutes that deep smoke of cigarettes in the accentuate cheeks, the voice grayly tinged, and the quick sips of café and. Quick coins. Always wrought by language this language, by *langue*, snare with what hidden byways shelved with concepts. Such movement and image it seldom forms speech but spells before exit, the object of desire. You know all this, have visited, peering over the pages, past the longing grip of that cover, restless for the object of desire.

CLOISONNÉ: THE VOICE INDICATIVE

With such black, he paints an outline of intent; hair stands, raised
from the surface of skin; the wind blows across the precipice ('Stand
back, let be, don't worry,' he thinks, thinks about telling her). She
looks, the frame she makes
of him, circuitous, angular, tongue-groove, a carpenter's awl; tongue
explores, moves deliberately
sees across all surface, wetness with tint (he as painter,

commands audience and critic and world and she: She's sprawled on the
freeze, a boudoir couch, right leg her right leg drapes over the edge,
an amulet, satin, where she would be asleep behind the dark silhouette a fan
might make) of him

his regard. His regard.
And when, some years later, he appears in this spot, jailed by bars of
light upon the parquet, the museum foyer, opening to this grand white
card, says invitation to his retrospective of paintings. There is a
shock, the circuit,
his wrist aches the worst burden he imagines her tongue, her
the deliberations of that surface: a wind blows,
hair stands on edge, even pulls, as stiff grass
on the cliff, a precipitous frame.

'A little, a little further back,' he urges her, moving the shiny
surface of his hand through the dark bristles, his hair.

There is the clatter of feet, the chatter.

UTRILLO

1

To grasp the flag
     /
of what is seen,   a thought.

Light = a cube, such sight, and that which plays
upon each quadrilinear plane, at all times, that be
the everlasting: take hands,
which turn and hurt with the crisp odour of crumbling black ash,
all the simple whole,
turn to charcoal, move to alabaster
to (the wrists, they swivel, no?)
that white-out la neige tone upon palette
such in turning hands, is precisely
a creamy beige, such thing as a pure-white?
Hold it up to the light, then. That pain,
turning grey of hand, wrist, always advance.
It is, it is the grasp: cool demi-tasse of coffee.

2

In hand, pulling out afterwards, or
the wrist's equatorial tension;

the hair left in the bristles
of a brush pulled stiffly
through
 each day. And in the mirror, it is today,
there it is, that, it's framed.

3

Scene i[17]

A window. No! So, what frame
and what gilding, then? Not even a breeze from,
the calligraphic Zen-guy's 'aha.'
Pencil! in quick hand, on the
other hand, precision of a draughtsman
in this glass cube is what one is if, and quadrilinear
spin real fast a dervish and that's much chills,
brrr—rr; the cubicle's frigid, like
an ice-cube indeed, the deep-freeze,
making the human body last and last and
that's where one is, one's words, the quick-a-graph
(the ology from 'deep') from every angle zap and hey
one's centred, eternal, *man*.

Scene ii

'Can I try this on?'

'Certainly. The change room's just over there, sir.'

And how fast undoing buttons,
in this cubicle, a three-way mirror, no less.
Meanwhile, outside, cars speed through grey snow,
ignorant of your antics, same goes for their drivers,
'no matter what way you look at it.'

Scene iii

Meanwhile, how fast, undoing those buttons
in this change room,
step back a bit from the mirror,
a good perspective, turn, one's got
a good view of the back too, it falls
nicely, is the thought,
'It falls rather nicely, sir.'
  'Oh. You. It's you. It's mainly wool?' And it is you
this sight, at least momentarily, at least momentarily,
burnt bones taste not so bad,
clear as ash, a white ash, as snow,
from another angle, you see it as gray,
this all-weather, impermeable garment.

November 8

It has started once more, some minutes ago, this rain. The pools again actively pour in the streets and thus past them these steps to retreat indoors. Here you enter with the merely damp now that damp permeates satchels, papers dampen, leaflets in valise be always what which one must periodically touch in the course of active life. Feet find no rest in these sodden socks, sodden shoes. The rain so lightly drizzles, as such crystals and traffic signals with all reason, change, constantly so. Halfway between decision and act, the cars (and she) which speed across the diamond of intersection signals to point for later reference (the memory). The memory will keep now its pointed invective, that
narrow tall heel that which twisted off the curb ('O-là-là'), like seance — as then, she turned you seeing, that head gestured back, that quirky annoyed expression 'Yes?' which barely lasts.
The neck.

'O-là-là.'
And here indoors, the smoke of cigarettes. Smells of seafood steamed to just there in fumé blanc fumet, defined with fragments of the laurel fresh in parchment (draws attention, retains its juices) the napkin of here placed deliberately as comma over the waiter's black sleeve, the hanging fabric lamps somewhat hobbyist's tiffany-style, the glass-topped wooden brasserie tables, the beige herringbone velour swivel chairs, *nicely* placed: sniff unconscious sniff breathe all in secondly to ascertain, then that constant clatter of cutlery, the
straight-back lean of such he is, again and again, rhythmic-repetitive, laying down the cups and saucers, the glasses — clack, clack, clack: the waiter times the waiter.

And everywhere as example, a gesture, she who has entered, is as much as incident here, specific remark her here where the lives of Parisiens push with taste electric and savour, O, the form of reverse (*Rive Gauche* and *Rive Droite*), boredom, agitation, the rigidity and movement flex note on her lips. The rural mind, a mind place in the city, the province all origin moving beyond its frontiers, returning only to the need, August green of vacation — one month — it's standard, leaves Paris, the architecture empty.

But now they, like her, have re-entered this place, the sweep of dry leaves, snap the autumn twigs, the Blacks holding the bundled-twig brooms. She is here, and you figured her here, the way the hand barely covered (your eyes the deign of pursuit) the mouth in that pose of average interest in *croque monsieur* or *hot dog*, elbow anchored by her inertia, or that comfort, that look. Impression, that look, that way the heel before broke the silence, could say — the way accidents make speech, or did.

Now, you could hope the perfume of seafood (a few unfinished plates) and melted gratinée emmenthal would unlinger here, but look, this happens: the soirée of clack-clack *marquee*, marquée of *sense*, that which stopping the accident of speech, you have silence, you have no way to write to the other(s) about this to say, 'Look here, my friends: reflection of lamplight on the glass tabletop and she, hand barely covering the mouth.' All average passes. Silence broken by accident. Without guarantee.

The traffic signals are rendered meaningless as accounts are given to the police who, arrive, the fragments of glass, the red and green beacons of control on and off, now the dampness of night lingers beneath table in syntax of, your legs which you cross which and the traffic all around must wait with exhaust for the passage an intersection extends.

PARIS: NIGHT AS SCULPTOR

It forms what night
performs, as
the voice in throat, the phlegm interrogative

throws to others —— what it's like, like the webbing
unstrung café chairs
     facing outward, there's the

 strong divan, the heartbeat.

Night's the throw, the other —— lingering
of cars' passing lights
only peripheral
in sight, as such integrity, seductive lines from
verse or

of times, each coffee the same, this place or others
remembered but fragments, to a similar feeling.

Sculpture displaces place
its medium in air,
night performs

like this wilful voice, wanting to what?
leaving here such taste,
leaving margins here and there

for the scan of auditory eyes.

DECEMBER 6 — RUE DE RIVOLI, MÉTRO: CHATELET

Who then, is that strong stranger I wish to know? Seated in that corner beneath the glow of tulip lamps, his head frozen in a single position, always at the cleanest table, his face is one I've known before. The waiter approaches, snaps down the dark strong coffee, a small cup decorated with pink morning glories, its green vinous leaves, the saucer chipped at one point on its gently faded gold rim. I rotate the saucer — perhaps ninety degrees to the right, perhaps — and I want to fold this page, this tale with its café, and as my tongue searches upon my gums, I long the dress to move such event to another restuarant where the waiter is more welcoming, more exact and discriminate; my hands prayed together, then butterfly, disclosing the logic of a newspaper's next page. I do not want this smell of demies, the beer spilling over rims onto shiny marbled tabletops, nor evening cologne. I do not want the show of plexiglass, nor tulip lights. The voices pitch panachée, a spill.

He is there: the strong stranger. Frequent, the announcements of exotic ice creams and sorbets — mangue and fruit de la passion — liqueur-wetted sundaes — poire belle hélène, coupe des îles — with cartoonish umbrella appointments on the glossy menu's front.

He is breathing (the chairs) at a controlled pace, his hat-brim folded over. But I want more — more than this speechless unsatisfying charade: this drole symbol.

Each time I set foot in this place, the same. The jim of speech stiffens within itself, a silence made of clamour, jam of pinballs and cash registers, the turning pages of a telephone directory; and like such waiter's cash receipt, there is a brief fiction, a totalling of account, aching its numerical rhythm against the terrace glass discredited with painted sign, the floors moaning under the weight of service traffic, patrons and the flash of headlights from passing vehicles splashing to mirrored uncharmed walls. In the stiffening of speech, there is dry change to breath, lifting this hand a tenebrious talc of defeat.

I can feel the shifts of weight as patrons slide in and out, Samaritaine[18] packages in hand, across the tensing floor, a cat's mating backs, the grievance of waiters as they enter kitchen carrying complaint: the doors sprung open, 'Hurry, I need that omelette immediately!' they will yell — at least they, heard above the steel ball collisions of frenzied machines. And I tremble again tremble, the want to turn the page, to move to more refined quarters of sustenance, to tear in fact this page of the night, take it undressing more stranger to bed, and begin. And begin the long melodic conversation over the dark pill of coffee, a plate of cold buttered toast, written in moody neon light.

FALLING OFF, OR THE HELD
for bp & Ellie Nichol

And around the spindle one
collects the simple limit of each breath:
 inhale / exhale, action it's all, is
interchangeably, a robin's brilliant departure
from branch, a cashier's punch on register keys
or letter, say 'f' or 'p' plucked
from the kinder's alphabet,

all which burns at vortex, maybe mercury ascending,
the hot hot breath, one to the next.

Starts, of course, as child, we spin the top,
or paddle red rubber rubber; and
in later years, our development, now even watch
the left wingers come in
on goal, slapshot or poke-
check just in time: or, Paris
or Dijon, it's *circulation* translating
the Canadian *traffic*, such spinning
speech, such roundabout where, light
or regular shadows fall across commercial streets,
4:30 sun radiant in these clear, cutting
December skies.

Everything collects, piles up in heaps: stones,
and minerals, dustbins and tors,
recycled bottles or secondhand clothes

      take again the top/spin's
   release: motions, potions, options,
etceteras spindle can hear its singing high-pitch
'All around the vortex we go ...'

... the crackling fire, smell woodlot, softening,
warming from crusty snow
in the fireplace hush. We count each crackle
as word, damp feet drying
and
all the friends gathered round the vortex,
listening to each other,
pinioned run of speech,

and perhaps it be only strep, hoarse throat,
not at all clear, this feverish imagination,
it's this
hot hot breath
heading, heading
into the turn of
the year,

    this Christmas,

just don't know.

MOVEMENTS IN A FORMAL LANDSCAPE: THE ATHLETIC

1

I am then, receipt and danger, a cap-opened pen on the fringes of the flickering bush. The brush moves through damp hair even before the morning coffee pot, drips of freshly drawn cold water on its side, is set upon the fire. And here in this garden, a wire traverses and for an instant, a leaf hangs precipitously, that electric power. Shock: a universe of flipped coins, rains the back of the hand, which can receive all, straightening the spine. Here is danger.

The sweep of natural-bristle broom across the garden dust.

2

He is eating lunch in the corner, every corner, portals, lintels, columns, dust: they fall everywhere open where he is eating lunch, a metal chair reserved for transient strangers. 'Cheese too firm, not warm enough,' he mutters audibly to self.
Wine tucked in a pocket, there is the shelf enough, arranged with bottles in a store. Stories blow past, under, through with the dust, some grit which ends in his cheese. They each oscilllate with worlds of purchase and exchange, the incandescent light bulb, the television VCR. Publicity. The cheese, controlled appellation from Normandy, cows' milk, 'a little too salty, but a good nut and straw scent,' he thinks to himself. The portals, the lintels, he now tones and braces himself, uncorks the bottle.

3

Rush and break away, rush and break away: stick and ball, carry it all or even empty-handed rush, and break away from the onslaught whatever that be, and no thought really of MVP, a headline, that kind of thing, even.

4

Training the mind so that the eyes start to close (and somebody's looking — at what? Looking at me?). Training the mind. Eyes starting to close, now you're getting the idea. There is protective railing. Guard dogs, trained, no less, which bite the hand of any OM, try to force, force eyes blink. One's eyes, getting thin and black now, getting there, one hears conversation of two (possibly retraction, one from other, looking at, at).

THE PONT NEUF
   for Stephen and Maureen Scobie

The point is
that, a new one way, to jump next
to, the from here and
that which, an interesting proposition
that which I can taste as *fort* as
something sautéed just to the point
of it, so suddenly, and a love for this,
all this place, big as a cow,
that is the point is
a departure is that new that's what
I'm sighing a sign
it's new the always
the Pont is new.

   b. (crystal)

Wrapped and un-
wrapped, shining heart
with Christo[19]
un rivering gift wear
the wrapture sol-soleil-
so sequinned ! dressed

   to-the-9s.

THE MEASURED MOVEMENTS: THE JEU DE PAUME

1

against against,

hands in pocket
against the wind, against the grey sea,
held

    in pocket
 leaves fallen   hands

hold the road
/to Louveciennes.

Transit>

   arms outstretched: arrow,
     coda, pigment

a)

hat tossed to sea
takes the wind
in its brim;

rolling surf white, white

 and ears rest
with desire.

b)

the boat afar a-sail, it makes the sound
of a narrow pin.

it is dying, the horizon:
the pen is held straight to its task.

Covet the family's support, and the
talk upon the beach
is drowned by the bleach of desire.

2

hidden under the bough
of flowers and verdure
the place of lunches and
delighted word
/in secret, place
to lay hat down,
to build the *strong* faith, upright
before seated evening meal,
place to make enigmas in,
there the casting rayon of friend
and talk.

(advance)

walk along the wall
or stone row,
it curves

or wallow
the hesitations
the hollow, the hillside of red poppies,
the straw hat is where
you placed it.

3 (Degas)

it is as if —
the metaphor, the lean
gesture: balanced
on a naked foot or
slippered — when light
touches and burns
the speech accidental
bright (sight).

      or

muscular action
in toned of forearm
strength that pressure
point on a sponge or cloth
to smooth the creased,
the heat of iron
in what one sees.
                         the will to focus

thought though, splayed out
a glance
such dance:
 to rehearse, to perfect
 with intelligent ear.

and not all
fully coloured fully noticed

fully figured
or toned,
 to press,

one must hold patient
a table

table

Gloss

And remember, an instruction,
a dancemaster waits to watch result,

adherence makes a foot cry 'foot'
stepped on sidewalk dog shit,
same the discarded spearmint gum.

4

there is the way action dies
at blistered mouth

this man, as an example
black folded umbrella
in hand, walking away
from these lips

the black leather of the
heels of his shoes.

leaving the scraped
carol,

that blunt crescent burn
upon this parquet,

5

up and down, and
that infant in next room
cries.

mouth open she

it feeds, that round hollow
one hears

back into night,
her gown.

(the way she kneels
at first naked,

back arching
 to the floor.)

6

A letter she was reading at the dining-room table

it was when you were small,
in that dark corridor, the hands
held in pocket,
the shine of hardwood floors,
smell of wax and
thereafter the
afternoon later
thereafter.

DETOUR OF A WOMAN
for Jacques Rancourt[20]

(AFTER A POEM BY MOHAMED DIB)

a pencil collected
in the hands, over
the substance of nights

a pen inexhaustible
with an avalanche of seconds, in
the writer's sight fixed

and everything in this unfolding plume,
feeding a reprieve
living as running
can

and suddenly, in
the bed's linens this writer
if not all, can place
a woman
 suddenly,
so voracious,
    but
    barely.

a light azure,
the filling winds
snap.

RUE D'ALESIA, 75014 PARIS

It all hurts the shoes
← →
they pinch the day away
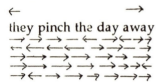

THE BRIDGE

a)

Who wants to speak — this morning, this afternoon, this evening,
this night — ?
Whose wish

like this, that, or that
that assured grin, push with the finger
at the bridge of the nose,
glasses,

    feel the weight
stand there, attending, of knowing
chance the risk and

out there from between
these eyes, glasses pushed again by finger on
the bridge say, overlook

their starched white shirts, the polished black calfskin
shoes, briefcases to match, weighty as navy
with red-stripe tie, its knot makes at the throat,
transactions of business bound into words,

easy chatter (laughter) at the bar, the cigarette
known by the relaxed hands fore and middle fingers,
as it moves assuredly a grin-arc to exhale
so easily betwixt words, throat-clearing
deletions
speech like that has not colour to remember
mark my own hand with reminder and

what is it like this, that or that
he's moved again a sale well-done with chatter forever

my throat,
speak, another on ice, who then? Who wants?

b)

Who then? He.
'Tee-hee' of comics,

a concealed voice appears
a bubble,
assured lines mark .
                  :
                  .

'he's a good actor'
'he's got the comic in him'

to make defence, mask for
privacy a goalie of
crossed words, high sticking or crossed sticks
atop the sleeves of a team jacket, hands,
they cross the face of the fence.

THOUGHTS ON CONVENTIONS OF STAGING

There are enough prospects, stages for concealed voice(s) the curtains traceably swaying, players to suggest the strength of these assured lines. Concentrate on wooden parquet, not faces, their lined skin, hidden beneath cosmetic (for layering found here) where the hand has held the privacy of thought long enough to make defence. And yet, there are prospects, these rigid against detention of the shades one wants to draw, doubling the drapery. But where out of this frame which evolves sign by sign, face by face, line by line, where can we pull the cord tight until the choke is complete and we need not parlay our admissions of throat?

We struggle here, that constant problem of shutting what need be open. Where are the knots, where can I overlap as a windsor and secure the resolution of crossed words which make naught when they cross, the tie of convention, the navy one hanging by the mirror, it has red stripes.

ON INTERIOR LIGHTING

A fire, as delicate as it is constant of small wax candle flames, encased in quiet red glass, pitched in lean towards the cool open doors.

Fire, as delicate as it be constant, is anchorage of this place, with its fixed geometry of marble floor, the fast figuration of hard-back cane chairs. (In another domain, insects are intermittent night-rain on the windshield of a car taking visitors home to the country). Voices of commerce, the ignition of vehicles, are held aback to the exterior, do not penetrate the geometry of chairs, and precisely, of the illumination of candles, their red glass cups placed verily on round tables, evenly spaced: they proceed to their bottom-wick. Such candles leaning towards the open doors held, cast an angle of their wane on sand-grey columns, a desert sculpture aligning its space. Words which emit here, like the fleeting thought of those country passengers home, know each day's damage, the way fire destroys in its architecture of space, with its transient angularity, the instants of memory.

DES TÊTES ESPAGNOLES

The way the dark sea-green
cannot tell you, my dear, of the horizon. Your breath,
your paragraph!

This hand shakes as one grabs the last food
from the hat.
One hand gives to vise the light
it be dark eve.

There are others of us, all of, with our hands
stretched out we touch each other
flesh and cloth to other flesh and cloth
at every point,

but there is no escaping
in the dark green sea.

Head tossed away
it lies far away from its neck,
it lies with its grin
it is in its velvet-lined cradle:
that is thought,   I see it is my education
  has done this.

The word missing.
Earrings, a necklace
gift-wrapped? A box?

Adherence:

Eyes with a twin to a time
of reunion with the colour of the frame
it will meet one day (like a gypsy coincidence)
(foretold yes?) it will hurt
cross paths again there entwined
keep eyes fixed straight within
to the road-sea
pain to a stranger rests comfortably in the bag.

Within your hands, can feel the,
empty as it's 'that much' but what's
there is the frozen act just parenthetical
but her last breath, tresses, a horse's tail
you knew wraps your mouth silent, silently and

what you're wearing,
of course, the cloth
such cloak and your dog standing
on your head, man's best friend could scratch
your eyes out, but sits obedient, trained,
and these raiments of the muse,
the terror of words
  you don't have it,

shortness of breath
coughing up the steak
that entrecôte

    chew it, is,
      it comes.

What's on the shelf?
Used, or decoration.
Get up early for the best flea-market
finds, or sleep in, the shit waking up
to the skull on the bedpost.

THE BARON HAUSSMANN

The Grands Boulevards, straight and harmonious, filled with the sunny emptiness of days in repose, when the people have gone. The trees, true down these avenues presence silent comfort a practised ease and thus, invitation to think while cutting this hour with walk not talk. As such on Spadina, in Toronto, that avenue I know, its own wide walks upon which I'd played hockey and ball. Here, as graces so easily into, the 'old shoes,' without bronze and such are they streets we find self onto and beyond now, the dark groping for speech to cover now, a tracery sound. One flits across shape, the clinging to body of transparent hose sheathing such litany of passing matter in fabric spun — that which refracts that constant changing light. *Pingping! Kacha-kacha, ping-pa!*

A small market street closed for the afternoon, tranquil; the coloured banners across the intersection, and the children at hopscotch, who then break, sit drinkless, needless too, unperturbed at empty café tables. Parole same time too, in a crowd, vowels and consonants gathered around the bar or clash the kacha speakers' speech ping play — pinball smack of small steel balls, machines and lights and polished glass. (The Grand Boulevards, straight and harmonious, filled with the sunny emptiness of days in repose, when the people have gone.)

The boulevard Haussmann, the boulevard Malesherbes! They do lead so on into the quiet interiors of shapeful desire of pronounced elocution of the muscle private, the heart. A want upon this place, the refracted spun of here, I want then this city, when the public is private, dressed in windbreakers or ties and creased cotton white shirts, they cleaning their motorbike engines, the metal shutters pulled down over the butcher's door, in the blood-wet aprons of this hour's rudimentary tasks.

A truffle in its package: The market of rue Treilard

Spun, it be like light so even, whirl the young girl who spins the street, that skirt blown upward to chin as gust is scent, that which reveals her undergarment white on form. A church door is likely opening, whereupon the tourists come out their cameras swaying and we enter the scene we centre and — our hearts street-smart, well-read are wrapped, wrapped. The sweet dark truffle purchased it was upon the sunny boulevard Haussmann, near but away from the hawkers their crowds outside the grands magasins. Unwrap the sweet: a single bite, not all, a wetness does not describe the concentration, the force at the table of repose, the cigarette smoke called 'late afternoon,' it be perfume of busy counter, branch of Saturday, drawing in the overcast, the filed-away sun. It disappeared sweetly, with a gust, before gentle voyeur could hold onto such light.

*

'Love, you have scarred me. It is reminder, the scratches I follow in design of that dust upon a windowpane, that which marks the invitation of spring.'

I've just finished reading this, and have withdrawn to this place, with its simple table and chair. The door firmly shut behind. The library silent as its signs command, adjusts its orderly shelves. I've retreated from a book's back cover, dust jacket in place where there be one, shutting the volume tight.

It is the mind in trace, flooded with velocity, speed which in end makes yellow to the trace: as one scans the olive-crusted hills. The map held with smooth dexterity of mind, or textured in scar of ruin or near-ruin at least, on clay, baked in hot sun, the map of topological stains, when hands touch a jug or vase. The take of sips of coffee from morning mug, accentuate the nerves of the hand, the context made within wrist, your and your eyes pitched downward in casual or causal cast, that hesitation between, in a lovers' discourse, each then looks carefully at the quotidian stains that pool in mugs called volume, the map of words or no words, eyes meeting pages, sanctity in divorce.

STUDY IN FORM: THE LOUVRE

1

Noun:

headless, aligned ahead in straight
where at noise, edges drop away
from hands
outstretched ...

       walk, walk there: a placement
       or what be   the story's

the etch on the body,
words, or seamless directions, borne
without edge, most rooted and whole
arabesque sounds; you have there

animals held in those very same palms.

These
(narrative of bottles,
stone tablets, tabernacles, there are glass vases
with heads of birds, and tails of handles gold) (I am)
dazed.

This head fully, of
'dazed,' assembling coherence, but
this diamond sutra:

136 karat it reads, of such dispatch of grand but
usual light.
        Or, beneath

the carved ceiling then, the position of hands,
gold hands upon golden lyres; besides the muscular
definitions of painted figures they territorially
contain in frame, what do they show, as for is the
flash of camera to capture, to years later, come
upon in a text?
Or,

a museum being washed after years, additions built —
all good as perches for pigeons e grackles — fly, fly. or
the shit! Wash again the stone;

and all the weight of this which
I am a part if at least
because I have heard and I read, am reading,
have read forming the particles of belief
that shimmering parchment: still

common sun in grey sky skits the river
beneath arched bridge, traffic
of cars, buses constantly turning at red lights
ahead. There or here (so much display
in labelled funereal chamber), we
so small the give-off of light
from this diamond stone of a scent.

2

After all the mind's quizzing of what to do, what café to sit in, where to eat
— the heart needs take its rest and it comes when one knows not a place
which could so feed.

Ancient Museum (1792). The Gallery of Apollo in its gold, (the Louvre d'or)
sets the fire beneath the tongue, the tingle that sense of shirt pulled up from
behind, from woo the tuck in pants — displaced, put disarray splayed
where one tries one tries to plant the feet, the feet to   set flame   to the
bank of worry.   Heart does push outward to catch prismatic view.

3

The thought, eh,

strewn — bread crumbs
fallen into the splice
of wood —

melon rind, gourd (the green,
yellow
            and the frail broom, still:

it is the gaze from that corner,
or the telephone call reaching
into the
night
your chest
the alarm,

        dressed wound,

    moon's shimmer on dresser, the heart
(your hand
reaching)
      hand on

         porcelain

         porcelain,

grip.

A Gloss:

Descendance,

 a tendency of us (parented) all, that is what is
parched in the throat of a millennium
of comings and goings, cinema evenings, cocktail kirs,
the squeaking of rubber soles, tell a tale over thousands
again on the marble floors the geometry which makes an
architect's plan (for monument, vestibule) into
the count of relax, work some more,
design, it was this other, now let us remember,
a delay, we're trying to connect the lexical number
to the illustration in the catalogue or guide, say,
 a sign.

Interlude:

that forgotten scene
behind this easel
behind the bold
laughter and guitar held in hands the turn
of the
hat-brim
the wind
  /
 dance when she
 arrives on your tongue
 and paint
 and varnish

that forgotten scene

of rowing, the grey waters, trees, flat —
   thought undescent

  dent

 of rowing

BREEZE.

4

There are three of us:
silent.

The meal

or robe,
or linen, mending.

Written. Woven.
Six hands make three

of us,

secret. Whispers
but none of us,
none

/ears

can hear.

5

That forgotten scene.

Rowing,   shimmers therefore

the grey waters,
trees flatten on
a corner, a spit,
a point

in mind feels

'furu-furu, furu-furu.'

6

Delacroix:

that lake that last boat

tossed,   coin

all floating, eyes cast up that last integer.

Capsized. Coin, O sun —

                                    hat tossed,

away the wind.

and the way memory comes
to form a title,

(Roma: 2 years ago)

ROMA: 2 YEARS AGO

In crowded cafeteria,
smell of espresso
on walls of the Galleria d'arte
moderna,

then,
brushed against / a grey
suit of worsted wool,
turn, shrug, that feel

at right shoulder, the contact
brushed the way you are led out
where

espresso fills the nose
the wind in the painting
it is called in its parentheses,
'Roma: 2 years ago ...'

7
 for Tamsin Clark

eyes led out. like thread,
touch filament,
this gossamer a river winds
on a Sunday

that translucent
touch comes grace off
the fingers,
so light from child.

7A

        so thread eyes,
     fine. do not
think but
recline.

8

Delacroix / Venziano

What is spelled down the robe,
the origin,
the tongue, grace
of look at,
what's glistenant
to come here.

That this takes her gaze
and soft palm (lifted to cheek
for she has
born,
　this Bright.

SOME VIEWS OF PARIS

Landscape

So it is again dear friend, fellow drinker of warm beverage, that we have come to such pleasant rest in this gentle garden of grey stones and well-set grass, where if we are moved, we can trace with ease, such circuit made by our steps, hand in hand we would advance, past the rows of scarlet hyacinths which give us even now such pleasure, which lead us on in ways we have forgotten but liked before. Negligence one could call the domain here, a place where pebbles and gravel take the weight of our bodies, they change composition under foot. Our usual thoughts have departed. We come again to mark our place with other strollers and Sunday joggers leaving untouched and silent the metal park chairs wet with the overnight mist. Dark brown leaves have fallen about the pillars, upon the grassy steps, and the sun has ribboned itself across the chairs. All activity is no different than in any park, and yet the movement seems to dissolve into a context as words develop a verse of something, like the current of air one realizes as breeze. It is for us to drink invitation, whether here or in another lieu — perhaps a day before, and either indoors or out. It is for us a dissolution of the voices until one hears only a singular voice distinct in its clarity from among all the stone figures built into this scene: the woman is frozen, is chiselled, and looking beyond; and she no longer thinks upon the lion by her side, head ungnawing, turned to our eyes: the lion without memory can be any longer neither queen nor king; a lion, a lioness as merely attendant, if you will. Dear friend, this day is not special from others we have shared together with our recurrent mild thirsts: pigeons, same as we've seen everywhere, they could even be split-shot destroyed in their clay flight: let us take aim. What we love in this park is the growth of our constancy and precision in what makes aright. We are avid together, we are Sunday drives past thistle and clover, and we are picnics there, a photograph which is found among the leaves, like those which could have blown under a porch. The porch is the base upon which resides gentle nostalgias, and it needs painting its grey back, where it is chipping and peeling away. No matter, all family members are grouped thereupon or thereabouts on the steps, the smoke of cigarettes, coffee mugs are apparent as another pigeon is shattered mid-air, in a sky around us most fabulous.

The Plan

In its every thing, is one at once located, how place insists its name. I do locate this city everywhere with its implicit time-quartered map. I am walking from Notre Dame towards the Pont de la Tournelle and then the Bastille, past the bordering concrete walls of the Seine; or seated for seemingly endless minutes with a coffee at L'Atrium on the boulevard St. Germain; the two avocados dix francs m'sieur, they are sold in the Métro stations en route to home after work; and here, in shops and cafés, everywhere that sawdust to capture the refuse and dirt is pushed away. Always the places, their objects have their light airborne with possible dust, or reflection stilled in a window just there.

The clatter of glasses or pinballs signal no particular nights or cafés of charm, but the talk of suburban residents out for a drink or the remedies of lottery numbers, not in some fin de siècle brasserie shine, but the spacious, rambling and new, this decade's vivid trying to be otherwise, where interior architecture is defence. Here is a café with its crowd of green plants so ambitiously placed, the odour of frites, the drums of a music enough modern from a juke-box played without stop, and a lighting intensely brilliant to install a world eclipsing fluorescence, with a fellow's harmonious sweatshirt certainly baggy, in evening blue and maroon, my own trousers properly pleated to style, the organization of cadre mechanical and spiritual, with smell and taste for one's innermost cravings, for interiors co-opted.

There are few modern vistas as defiant in their scale as La Défense; yet, I come here willingly, to relive such cinema scenes, say, with
Alain Delon, scenes of descents from a speeding
Renault which hastens to
sudden park, the then drinking of demie or panachée beer at a bar with guarded or congenial barman, the headlights and red tail-lights of speeding cars.

Do I know where to stop? he wonders. I write,
the spread of this page on a table too common, the clawing shadow of an overhanging green plant. Precisely where narratives come to a forget, the second step surmounted without trace, the incidents occur, and the hands in jeans pockets, blue and maroon sweatshirt of mode, are accidents and danger. O good danger though, they have no more remaining of that plat du jour, the elimination of choice. The waiters are insistent, coming back always, always there, the light is well, heavy, giving faces ambiguous charm. The juke-box music advances from background, ambient cap you are wearing: Lionel Ritchie, Lionel Ritchie with a song that is magnetically popular, it's that cool imported, easy American soul.

It is precisely the piston of narrative drive. The daily special of which none remains, the menu page replaced each day, telephone is ringing. In Canada, Barrie, Midland, or Niagara Falls — the Horseshoe Falls — that wonder of wonders in Ontario, the telephone is ringing at a basement pay phone in a bar. The scenario says, a suicide plea to no one in particular, hopeful for attention; for an architect is sketching out his research of sadness, he is Paris with a dream, he is breathing his own notebook, his history, he is making a film.

I am the one abruptly at this bar, and detective with demie.

There is a car chase past the Place de la Concorde, and they are merging onto that road which makes perimetric circle around this city of dreams, a story with the speed of a chase on La Périphérique.

Lieu

I think of you now, in search for that quiet, that place next to, but detached in grace, from thought. The small chapel speaks a *fort* reassurance, but never it invades a heart, which honestly and humbly seeks peace. 'There are no solutions,' it will call with its mitred presence; and yet, comfort purely by its constancy, votive candles always in thoughts, a prayer unsaid but counted for brother dear He knows, always there and ready. The glorious rises from cold floors to the hands they paint kiss, kiss, kiss.

I am now in my own place of peace (it is the Church of the Madeleine), so much larger, grander with its rows and rows of empty pews and the odd, lovely clatter of footsteps on marble stone floors. Up above, small round windows the heart of painted jewelled domes yet, large enough to house all wound for their donate, this light. Seasons. The font, the sacred, semi-circular form and sculpted Madonna, well-witness. Such wonder that organ, the grand organ can fill this place and pour brimming the whole, sole body with thunder and deep lock, I can imagine Master Fauré,[21] his fingers on keyboard, his foot on pedal.

This place same, is so much the place for you. O, to not seek but purely take habit — with the others brightly seated even if dourly attired, each has reservation of place, it was destined sighless, in signless purpose in those builders' labouring hands. O, I know and love your place, but travel here. For I know, I believe rather, that in this season, as rain turns cold with autumn's descent, here is appointment and timing so fundamental to you, the gestures of your body in the slack of sound hope, with sacred music against a city's quotidian ravaging hunger.

Composition

A place so drummed and unrelentingly tensed, the cars full speed along the route of the Seine; and the trees by bridges which traverse the river, persist out of a grassless seeming humbug earth. Benches, half-fallen, are caught with the strikes of the sun, the warmth that parks in the repose of clochards, or those who quietly read with sure station, casting eyes intermittently upward, a cyclist perhaps to mark wheeling past, the composition somehow elegant.

In moments of overture which one yet ascertains is the good timing or clean climate, beguiled is the gloom of eclipsed emotional souvenir and the confused darkness of the most obvious and well-reasoned argument, they are in fact chauffeured to dispensation by the exhaust of cars. One comes upon another visitor on the grassless dusty terrain; and it could be as before a duel of muscle or wit, but it is rather the quaint gesture of a handshake. In this protraction of the good sweat of an architecture sublime, a palm, one to that other — the magical self, we look up ahead: a child is seen running after a flight-borne balloon, the composition somehow elegant.

Or, for the reader upon a bench, there comes a page torn in half, exposing a melancholy (romantic) removal. Thus is its signative accent say, like an emigré's, incomplete at best, is that perfect; and there too the sound-effects (SFX) of a cat replaces the real, that which is the not here; and that too, is a composition of elegance.

CHRIST EST PÊCHEUR

On a boat, I am dreaming in a painting by Georges Rouault (Paris 1871-1918), it is the *Christ est Pêcheur*. And to say that after entry, one mounted the two succeeding escalators to arrival and view, to the panels and walls of the site, a site established for the history of gestures of artists, of catalogues and postcards, of posters and lost and found. What's the news? There's the thickening and itching in the throat as usual, the self's promise then of liquid refreshment, undoubtedly coffee for so-and-so francs,

on a boat I am dreaming in a painting by Georges Rouault (Paris 1871-1918), it is the *Christ est Pêcheur*. That easy and summery, I think, I am on a porch, worms or wet cottagey rain or insect bites, green steel of an angler's tackle-box, small pliers and a #3 Mepps lure. Flashlight, coming back up the well-trodden path from the shored rowboat on North Milne Lake, here's the screen porch, my impulsive hand on Ros's hip: is Temagami, Northern Ontario, 'Pop would have liked this, wish he were here,' words cramped in ballpoint on a postcard even, I tell her, thinking 'his stomach cancer' no, not even that exactly, as I mark a desolate floating boat as I first sketch with water and pencil a possibility the North, as it's damn this floating — keyboard the clack! shutting of tackle-box, the screen door ferociously slamming shut, with its soft wood, its thin wire-mesh screen.

DECORATIVE

1

Upon each nail, is something hung: a towel, the wire which secures behind a painting, a cup slanting from its handle. A finger filed, so indecisive; a thumb filed, so deliberate. You've placed those heads, hammered into place, coloured them there, with such relative ouch.

2

(what are you saying, little boy?) Your mother behind you is watching. The old trellis covered with its hanging verdure. The white posies in the pot. There is drink. There is a story to read, book unattended. A fly seconds departed. The next chapter, fingerprint on a page, takes place in the garden. Let us take lunch beneath the measure of the comforting trellis.

The Lunch:

Poppies. Certainly, child seated in the shade, the white starched linen drapes beside him from the round table laid with fresh apricots. On a bench just to one side, baskets contain wildflowers gathered in the morning. Look to another, a basket of field snails, or perhaps taken from vines. I am hunchbacked for now, unwilling to proceed. I might write you again. Brilliant insertion.

THE POST-IMPRESSIONISTS

PISARRO

To pick twigs and leaves
dried by late morn sun
on the damp summer path,
 the woods of Barbizon;

or take to that smoke of distant fires,
season's dusk of sweet chestnuts from charcoal
on the stone terrace landing, you reach from
up the cobbled way, and speak
gently, to husband ear,

'in the woods of Barbizon ...'

VUILLARD

Through door ajar, the floral garden.
Rest with what's left to drink,
the garnet in carafon and sewing pins
à table. Fall asleep
until autumn comes;

and seated there, who is it
waiting for you in that place and time
throws the garden's,
the water's spray, upon drying yellow leaves?
Admiration between two sisters
who have aged in distant worlds:

you step into this place where
together we've pictured our years,
the colours so still
upon the painted dish.

PORTE D'AUTEUIL, PARIS 16ARR.

And now I am waiting the days to leave this place. I come to this quarter, to visit her and sometimes she is not there. I leave notes slipped under her door, and then sit here before catching once again the Métro. And I am waiting the days to get moving, spend my time in some other land.

```
                transit    >         to train
                              for Spain
                  keeps saying, keeps saying
                  'on, on, on, on, a, a, a
```

a.'
                                        a

The coins   (listen,
hands, hand in this, any dark pocket)   a   a

  rustle   a

all that is there
                                        a

b.

The coins

tossed,

   on table,   (away, away!)
dice: dots

The you gamble the clatter   scatter

y', your heart. The gamble loose change, you feel
in this city, the chamber, people, chamber. Hear,
close, ear
 as if (dark   hand
or head)   breath catch if
 as if, micro-
     phone: throw dice voice it
            comes back even closer, pocket as if 'a, a, a' mouth near
            wrapped around it, pops and fuzz

registered   recorded   condensed
now, is it that larger perception?

         transportation

c.

On table you gamble a Sunday a café terrasse, here at Porte d'Auteuil
as before and always hmmm? It will be
you anticipate,

: playing numbers, that's the way, now or coins clatter 'wish,'
the lottery the weekend-relax
and one of you yells 'Michel!' for another drink who
will it be

just totally relaxed with free time
(dark coins, no sun)

comme   zaaaaa.....!

d.

e.

Currency between you is not
tied to each oncoming wave of despair over kir, hachis parmentier,
France-Soir, each tide of the

petites annonces which leave their coins sounds like
ça, soft 'c'
troubled against the cold hard clash of this amplified heart, precious
infinitive, communication lines,

this lottery Sunday
waiting
the a-train
between numbers un-
painted
>

ARLES: AN ARTISTIC CONCERN

A walk through the lens:

    the pebble and saw, one stumbles not
    the fragrance of a stove's softening brunoise-
    la lavande, le muguet, l'olivier,
    le thymn, le pin, le basilic, la sarriette;

and through this noble house erected
on the noble stand of a hill
across the track, one viewed
a romance there. L'herbier, parfum,

        Postcards; Date, place —

delicate hand-made paper crumbles to one's travail. Creation.

A bench has been left to gather dust on its stone matter,
to become the table
of breadcrumbs, a picnic for birds; and then,
a chain of orderly tourists, ferreted by bus
and the pigeony announcements of a guide
appears before sun's scatter through past imperfect
the winnowy glade, the cascade of planes, pages
the arbours walled by years of poets and painters
those contemplative you-knows in stroll, aisled upon
the canisters which store flesh
and their testament bone.

2

Through a wire-mesh fence, water so still, fragrant with
the gather of dark reflection, tourist aside, and the scatter of seed
and dust.

Phew!

SPAIN

ALCAZAAR DE SAN JUAN

5 OR 6 P.M.

Yet, here with the moving of bodies, of families, so darkly, children in hand
and the night is not yet, the pink (dresses), pale blue (sweaters), exactly
pressed slacks and brushed hair and colognes spell the bright of this hour.

And then, this waiter in form's
control: white shirt & black vest,

wrist and hand
   /
two saucers, cups

are such balance, the principle,
the moon

a guess, dip

cold fingers know an ink;
       know as opposite, aching habit, the moon.

*

Knees touch, so close quarters of strangers
so close,

She?(looks)he(object)
'Cigarette?' a lighter which drops, rolls on floor
is not distraction.

Knees touch still
still feet so fixed (continuity) they could

toss in a sleep; the rest?
ash.

*

A uh.
A e.
A mm.
A ih.
A uh.

*

Upon the glass counter, the plates of sugary doughnuts, the crisp glazed puff-pastry palms and colognes flattened by evening air, spell the bright of this hour.

IV, FOUR

La Mancha plain, morning mist my robe.
Church simply red, cold
La Mancha.

Four days, digits
the count and
no reason (why this or that?)
as why the seasons are.

Small street, long street
heels on pavement, hard leather
and this morning's damp.

Four seasons: spring, summer, autumn
                 winter, this February so singular
                 to encompass all tell

four days. Now the sun is
through this mist, slight
radiance,

the 'crack' in a bone yet,
of this one hand

: train! February!

Station up ahead,

the arrived.

TO CORDOBA

1

Green grass. Arid yellow grass. Treed mountainside. White rock/stone, a wheel and the milling always or once the eyes. Eyes looking from this train. Slow vehicle this, on these tracks. Grist hands, hands of form. Could be hands of Christ. Simply form, the way of looking.

Aqueducts collect speech, there is this direction outwards. Wine in the glass, in the hand, or wash hung to dry. This is collected speech. She is (collect) dreaming of aqueducts, her river is flowing outwards. Now the scarlet, bleached, snapping in the wind.

2

The smell of fried hake never pushed from the swarthy lingering air of the streets, nor the sound of uneven walking, and maybe a popcorn cackle — birds, a limp; unperturbed, scent of oranges. The white walls opening to green, polished patios they hail to the echo of stones well-received and of TVs and then to pass that face of a church so shut an ochrous, rusted bell of colour. And so the throb knowing rain's preface, knowing night's nostalgia Allah open sesame only at Mass what doors Serrano ham hung to dry and the peeling sea-blue paint off walls.

Align self, good posture, signature on dotted line and don't piss in the alleyway please, and then again, the old metal chime from Mezquita, the Mosque: it is not loud, you are not far. The sky, even if clouded is low enough to be the roof, welcome of repose the way no need of retractable dome or planetarium sky with reclinable chairs' head rest to support a marketing or vice versa. Desire seats under a cushion of speech, the vertebra sings disco, sings even —
song. It's fun.

MEZQUITA

CORDOBA

The wooden benches covered in dust
what is formed in the arch
the curve of the mosaic jewel
pocks of light, reflect upon, dust formed and covered
   swept up by the woman, a pushbroom quietly
on the marble floors in the morning — swish-swish
or a workman's power saw, restoration of site — sywz-sywz!

She is wandering, map in hand, description
in hand, the footsteps and there's a wooden bench
flying up towards an arch — that one there,

tracing spirit she moves not, but is dancer
more than just slave to those words, but by
the guidance of light, as it ciphers
the dark.

Forest of pillars and arches, the air
remains cool light changing its
habit with window miraculous, superb, nifty or
'Let's pray; Let Us Pray' it describes the space by which
it's confined: or it's also a postcard you bought it,
I bought one and she

walks in this direction of sound, steers
away now from the black metal barriers
which prison the dark alcoves
with their paintings and secret worship, secret hues (prayer
                    such beautiful chance)

and a mumble is poetry, nonsense, speaking
in tongues, leafing through; and by the doctor/therapist, kind
of a 'Sir Michelin'

she is told to lose the self by the trace of a path
sketched by details
: numbers, colours,
the codices of
history (in fact)
buy the complete kit, paint
by number, take a package
winter vacation
to wooden benches covered in dust, the Islamic,
the Mudejar, discover other cultures
and use no erasers;

a broom.

5 . 2 . 85

I must sound like a romantic story; a tale enough maudlin to be sure. Rosy pink napery laid before me and coffee, dark, strong, small after dinner coffee at my lips. Do I now imagine the moon in the steady blue-black sky looming over me, this tented roof over the bell tower of the Mezquita, ancient mosque of Cordoba? I am almost thirty-five now: let's look at the watch, shall we? Just over an hour to go in the proscenium countdown.

The restaurante is empty but for me, it is so spacious, so dark woodish, so so Spanish, shall we say? But there is, I'm forgetting, the bar. The noise. General noise, drinks, you know, drinks being poured, drinks clink-clink and, little plates of tiny ripe green olives. And so, if I might enquire, what's with the taped waltz music, please? There is no flamenco in this Cordoba, which is not Vienna, nor Budapest, but winter. The *cante jondo* — the deep song ...

The *cante jondo*, so loved by Garcia Lorca, eh?

Here he is then,

    'Presenting ...' (this is my cue),

alone, for he can't speak Spanish, cannot talk (and yet, he is saying as if between the lines of his attempted meaning, his meaningful gestures as he orders his meal etcetera to the waiter who's another etcetera, 'Look, it's going to be my birthday,' and he expresses this rather gently).

    'Presenting, presenting ... '

    'Bravo! Uhhh ... Okay, you can go now,' he calls down,
    securing the final letters on the marquee.

Not so fast. You see, it should have been that his love was here, wagging her hand saying 'Present!' And she would reach across the table and breathe, 'Happy Birthday,' and 'What more can I say,' like he had said to her like she had to him in exchange the delicate breaths and sighs marking the inflections of twelve different years.

She continues, as he pulls at the yellow ribbon of the cute little packet, 'You know, now you're probably going to laugh at me or somethin' but, you know, each time your skin feels so good, so nice. I never ever get tired of it. Of that, if you know what I mean. I mean it.'

Reflections dance across the glass as I record this as quickly as the click of their steps, the snap of their fingers. And if you'd comment that a profile moved across the table linens ...

Ah, the waiter perhaps, with this kind of, it's such good service, so sympathetic. In such pathos, the waltz music now in reflection, seems, shall we gloss, somehow appropriate. Might I hasten to dismiss any possibility that drinking excessively of the ruby Valdepeñas wine has effected this compromise to ambience, to ambient sound. The decor of meal, the sense of the appropriate in reenactment.

Reader, there's some wine left in the bottle, go ahead, be my guest. The artist is rather insignificant, in a general sense, here. He is a visitor to Spain, without connection to the land, its spirit, its people, but really getting into it, though. His finger at the table, the pink napery of the meal, he getting flushed, seeks the apt page, their umbilical text, the just correct phrase of Berlitz, the way fingers might lightly, distractedly drum. He wears a backpack; he is wearing money: after all, a tourist at first glance and last, how we always depart a foreign place. He is in this picture, everything you want him to be: a rather silly story, with decent trim. On cue, parenthesis opening to the story, he writes a poem, draws a picture on a new page he's flipped to in his black hardback journal with lined pages which alternate with blank ones. The waiter looks, rather curiously, raises his eyebrows and walks away backwards. The small plates of green olives refreshed with seconds, morning edition snappily replacing the evening final. Goats climb the sierra.

The coffee cup so small is almost empty. The wine bottle remains one-third full. This is a question.

And then, he really did not want it this way, stiff upper lip and all that. And you, as you finally take the invitation to red wine could have cared less this maudlin thing, not terribly interesting except yet, and you love yets, (But what of his art? Indeed.) the heavy vanillin of oak barrels.

Olives crackle with their pimentos, a man at the bar claps sporadically a rhythm within a rhythm. The dancers you've not seen up to this point, fanning themselves with their orange and rosewater hands, mopping sweat off their brows, take a bow in their Straussian attire.

'O Gloss!' one shouts.

'Allah,' mumbles another in a muted duende[22] response.

The music's not so bad in this joint. Really. Eh? And the dinner was just fine. It was fine. Fine. The stomach full, grumbles with glee. I apologize for this simplicity, this picture — maybe I've interrupted you at your meal? He is still in love with her whose affections in the more profound way, have passed. She is dealing with her own life; it's her place not in this place, her elsewhere, after all.

GUADALQUIVIR

FEBRUARY 6, 1985

Beneath the full winter moon
lightly wrapped with cloud, the argument's
fish stills the mind: Essence; fluorescence
illuminate silent
parked cars; where here streets are no more
routes, but deep unquestioned tales let be
in afters of meal's taste — Aquarian
February; Cancerian February: grapes and pine nuts,
anglerfish and thick banana cream:
Guadalquivir under bridge silently
river's pushing
: it is the bridge, name's Roma.

There are no streets there are streets:
there are no cars there are cars: a koan
drops from oleander.
Night is a rest of pink glow
electric lamps cast upon monuments
and common concrete ground, they breathe
cool meaning.

Dust and matchstick night, watch, watch
still, smell of urine, stallion manure
which greet our robbers, our sleep-weary minds.
(Bell tower striking) Bell tower fades the night
quickly, 'quickly robbers!' who chance
who steal away the soul in the glassy pools,
the microbe-dropped seconds.

There are no cars there are cars,
there are Coca Cola signs, guard dogs too
in haven warehouses; there are
still even in sleep's sector of town,
revved engines, motorbike speed

                    /

                and yet general night is a thin pill
and with you, with you
I have knitted a pocket
and reserved a place
by this river.
And do I then, do you
with me my friend, dive
from this streetlight, this fluorescent
invitation, cast upon
bridge to town?

THE BREAKFAST OF SENECA

CORDOBA — FEBRUARY 1985

The clanging of the bells outside —
a knife-sharpener's?
Or, the starlings with breakfast crumbs
across the steeples turn a chain of keys
of cathedral scale, and here this voice
seems to trail off ...

    And all
the kinesis bound tightly in heart
(non-particular) resides within with the green,
green — palm and ochre tiles, geraniums;
oak table for breakfasts, and wisteria on these patio walls and
yes, lemons, bamboo.

    And all
above such enclosure, a square of open space this roof
from corner-point to corner-point, the sky; what's
framed?
And the canvas too tent-drawn and green across midday
it holds one in.

What is the ideal house, to speak,
inner court housing rapier or rest from contact with
surface, with the street,
dedicate to restless tongue, or tasting amber in which
'Cordoba! Hail Cordoba!' says that tawny, cask-drawn wine.

What openings are permitted to this place
private (as that which, up the sleeve?) for they welcome
the bells, the bell-ringer's hands, clear

as blade, his steel and
still, when it's said, 'in a pinch'
there be an automatic architecture of small and en-
closing fingers, yet heat of thought (the burning rad)
suggests yes there yet
could be that opening the. the. the. the.
The opening, is for some thing/other touching
muscular heart when
provoked by the
elements passing overhead in the
tented sky.

So, (one might say over breakfast, one says, says what? Too much,
too much is said, it be) only sky, with its sun, cloud,
rain and hard bread cradled in palm, coffee
at finger of other,
what we've named, uh, bread
say (the burning rad)
is a civilized word as fine as proper meal manners,
              classic and precise.

But here, in the plan of supping at night's table
the garlic fruits, a bull's stewed tail and torso
and dried mountain ham, hoof of course intact;
Moriles wine will salve the throat:
there is refusal to grant in space as such
 an openness to explore the openings, da the's, to
address naively the oleander, 'Greetings'
growing lazily by these walls,
it's making that start of day told
by bells. Bells.

WAR AND PEACE: THE TOREADOR

CORDOBA — FEBRUARY 1985

1

She holds a skull in her eyes
and around her the smiles, small
from the dark, gleam.
She turns and holds a forging cast
as if bronzed reflecting
the pencil of ombrous salon
the ache which you know, period;
in the cavity of the chest.

2

The funeral is flown with weeping,
and flowers, and cured-ham sandwiches, and
ripe fruit tossed across the threshold
of death — a family party
mourning in sunny plot in dusk
so gypsy imparts
a tune, withering
sunlight.

3

Her long dark hair falls a horse's tail across my face, I am the waiting one
and hope with her pale blue satin gift, her lace; and across her stomach, atop
her folded hands to the floor cascades the drying flowers, some, that same
blue which fades.

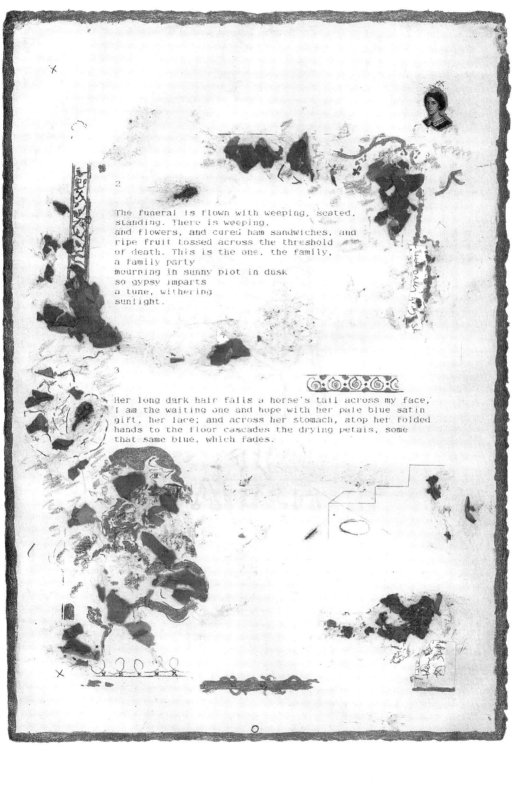

2

The funeral is flown with weeping, seated,
standing. There is weeping,
and flowers, and cured ham sandwiches, and
ripe fruit tossed across the threshold
of death. This is the one, the family,
a family party
mourning in sunny plot in dusk
so gypsy imparts
a tune, withering
sunlight.

3

Her long dark hair falls a horse's tail across my face,
I am the waiting one and hope with her pale blue satin
gift, her lace; and across her stomach, atop her folded
hands to the floor cascades the drying petals, some
that same blue, which fades.

4

It is nuclear night
a battlespring of thought, to twist
the fish of argument, to say
what's right and then happily carry on,
eating.

Describe the self
by painted or vocal lexicon
the ways a legend's told
 /that sweep of ordered tiles
against your sleep.

Sweep such withered blooms
and then bold and curt
as her thin band,
red ribbon tying back secured
of her bunned black hair,

>   her pale neck,
>   her repose.

It feeds you
in your explosion,
period.

ROMERO DE TORRES TA-TA 1987

'Sh-sh, she's sleeping a (or) dead,
touch her feet, I love you,' is my call, my repeat
to her. Give me your fingers, touch your dark nipple
will it rise hard for me?
                        'Shh—shhh—'
says she, another,
at her feet, her own nipples
so freely relaxed
beneath the sway of her sweet gown.

*

Naked, or almost, she's let down her black hair,
she's so gentle (I remember), holding
the skull, and wraps it with her own
tresses, the entwining curve
of her red-painted lips.

AT 8:17 EVENING, IN THE BODEGA RAFAE

When he picks up his glass tumbler of white coffee, the darkness passes and the caravan enters with its strong ivory horses, tents and fires burning into the night. The colour here, the scarlet the leaf greens suggest salads, embroidered upon shawl, flash through the tempered light, a woman approaching the bar. 'Yes?' asks the barman, 'Yes,' she says and 'Yes,' also this last one, the customer of the evening enjoins, almost his neck uh, 'I shall look behind me to that voice, I will advance,' thinks he, drone up from sleep, his fitful bachelor's pose. The ground of course, is littered with papers and toothpicks, the unemployed sing, and the patrons relax. But the caravan has left. And next — yes, across from him, the barman is wiping a slender sherry glass with a blood-stained cloth and the bachelor sees in this servant's eyes, the two dancers — one male, one female, upon a spotlit stage, and their heels are burning in the flames of a gypsy immolation tent. 'I will have *flammenquin* to-night, my man,' he tells him with familiar authority. His feet within polished black calf-leather shoes know the sweat of an infant's scarlet fever. The polish is fast, it will not stain. 'Do you expect the weather to change, sir? And when?' is the barman's polite yet incisive quiz as he cuts the first layers from his sweet hairy forearm, a sharp blade indeed in search for the dry haunch of inland mountain ham. And for his part, this patron whose elbows rest upon the wet and salt spill of the counter wood, is a young man growing forever younger by oscillate degrees, he is pushing with each second, his tumbler of coffee down the length of the bar, playing a seeming strategy game and pulling out the threads of leafy green blood, embroidered in his breast.

after:

'It's no good. Fuck,' or some such he shouted, spitting the squid onto the already littered counter. And at once too, the-hard-bread-ring-rebounded-off-the-wood-and-fell-to-the-floor-disappearing-into-the-deep-piles-of-paper-refuse-stained-with-lips-and-fragments-of-breath. He / scraped / the leaves / from / his / plate / and / drank / deeply / the / amber / wine. This was not the first time, nor the second, that such had taken place. Not even, the third.

SONG OF SPEECH

It is this room one wants, then. Or this corridor the want, this door,
or be this window, this corner definitive. This patio too, as much one
wants safety, as safe withholding the jewels of sign in calligraph's
verge in dust airborne, roots place and time, fashion fast.

                                                    That which is.

Sweep arm and hand across the air, that sweep, you say, this territory,
become you in gesture; wanting.

But such movement has been with study left behind and there / for the
wanting, that speech one might make from podium say, the, the words
which vainly fail in seminar forum, a vale, a room full of waiting
faces, cold sweat empty intestines ugh, have forgotten, behind you the
sweep of arm and hand across the air. It is you are now saying that
which is, it lies in next pose to next, say prose.

SONG OF PROSE

It is morning, neither early
nor late: and gay night has gone with today

              like 'dingle-dingle' a tin can
rolling down the street, no, 'ji-jan, ji-jan,' the rusted heavy church
bell clangs a constant space it divides. And all the while are there
always clippity footsteps in the streets they fill windows as bells do
the signals, as girls too are, notebooks in arms, their wire curly
coils, going to school and laughter. A yellow canary
pecks at its perch and sings its sharp 'till, till, till
tit-trill-til-and quick: whistle!' The butcher in his apron, looks out
to the street, it is morning, an apricot tumbles from a crate, and he
sharpens his blade, 'szwyh-szwyh!
           szwyh-szwyh!'

THE NEWEST OF NEW DREAMS, AND
THE MOST FOREIGN OF STRANGERS

What peace then that
reigns here, an embed of stone,
a sore tooth of music of
fountains risen up high.
White marble floors here, in this
garden. The small orange trees
tartness on tongue, the way
power of spirit speaks: the candid swim.

It is here embedded; the marble

neatly laid; fountain is gentle.
You speak quietly of a pedestal
covered with the hours of green moss.

      Covered / this
      excavation this relax
this flapping rhythm betwixt tribute and fatigue, of
white pigeons and starlings' wings: and back, against
a spout a small round, marble fountain.
Word when it was not
electric; stone. Was.

So much written here thick
with moss, still waters
in this eye, a pool.

There are windows, of air, of black
cut open spaces —
        enclosed. Here. It is dream
(so you should remember; perhaps write it down upon
rising; the carnation, hibiscus and that other would
bloom here) its scent aware aware[23] in oranges, but too,
the dark holes. Sarcophagus, the breath in stone, our gaze remains always,
directionless in lungs as much as our fingers
are first action then term.

Enclosed here in this garden
the still water is gypsy
the trickle from spout is gypsy
                           (sleep or medi-
                               tation: alarm?)
the penny drops)
the marble pedestals are mute
are broken in days and months
and white, etched, and with dirt
and too, green, green
green with moss,

perturb,

is eaten,
sunk in hole: musical signature,
walk   /walk the direction this post
of archaeology,
of constant trees
with oranges, the white marble like new
leading uniformly to the spout, can kind of *'name
that tune'*

    do you or I ask
what codes are on the ochre mean
of walls beside
in this garden
in this page or two
of season and spice thrusting
with the moss and marble
marble on the possibilities the square calm pool

— how gentle could be, or violent
    the throat!

BURNING

           damn dust and

sand, mosaics
broken   /see speech fragmented, in a way   hey lizard,

there is, large bowl of clay fused from sand
the fine diligent hairline pattern rising
or descending vertical: fingers of the hand. Whose

heart within this? Dust and shoes,
like yours in print (like dusty alley, you are
in or sand beach same a history?) Other-
wise,

mouldy oranges wet in garden soil.
Fallen,
mud and green-leafed tendrils, neighbours they are,
say.

One discovers more: another vase,
some dried peels of Seville, rather
Cordoban oranges
too one discovers more,
sand, sand is sand, can't say conjunctions of its grains, say,
words in the spout or pools awash there
is there.

Hey! High-pitched song-birds
above, though not the mountain.
Not God / car honking in

distant traffic: a heat could be,

come my friend we are we,

take my hand, please.

THE ASH

Warm and fragrant in the tree-lined air,
grasp the lemon, young ————> past peak, this fruit
it comes now to rain.

THIS IS ABOUT MEDITATION
   for David McFadden

CORDOBA, SPAIN

This is about meditation. It's what I realize. I sit here, and in front of me, I stare at the residual brown foam of coffee which stands now in broken cloud formations on the sides of the glass cup. Next to this glass cup, a spoon is stained in the cradle where coffee drips are wont to rest. This is about meditation in Cordoba. There are white pigeons constantly overhead: the singing of tiny birds in the tall palms, as well. A young couple wearing sunglasses in front of me are seated at another table. Her glasses are mirrored.

A pigeon has come to rest on high. Not in a palm, but at the top of a streetlamp, where it walks back and forth. I am reading a good book. I am getting hungry. Through my mind, images of deep-fried squid rings flash. I am not a good photographer; but I like to take pictures when on vacation. Coffee. Ah, it's the way I like it; and I return the glass cup to the table. I am reading a good book, though from time to time, I do raise my eyes. I like to take in context when on vacation. Singing birds. Still there. They are small.

The gypsies have this way of making money. It is not particularly aggressive. I have seen it in practice in the very nice pastry-cafés here, during the late afternoons. A small child is sent through a crowd holding a baby, and she stretches out her hand, begging for money. Sometimes it works; sometimes, it doesn't.

When she approaches me, I now, after some practice, have the strategy down pat. My instincts are sharp. My eyes never look directly. They are incredibly disinterested. I can shake my head in the 'no' pattern with wonderful conviction — so that it is final, in an instant. Flash! Got the picture? She goes away. It's o.k. — she'll, I'm sure, get loose change elsewhere. When people ask, I say I am not really political, though I tend to vote without exception, and side as it falls, to the left. 'I'm more anarchist,' I say. 'Actually, I act on spiritual beliefs,' I say. This is about meditation. If you wish, you can now go all the way back up and begin re-reading this piece.

'Duende' Lorca wrote — is that magical force or goblin spirit which exists in the best flamenco — when a dancer stretches beyond mere form. It is the white heat, the black sooty cool of the dusk calles of Andalusian life. Flamenco originated with the gypsies, their Moorish wandering spirit, smiles with death in the jaws. Can't you just hear the cantaor's wail right now?

Everything should be just dandy. I wonder (it's about the fourth time the question's crossed my mind) how much the two coffees I've had will cost me. I am reading a good book, I add: and you, well, of course ...

A Spanish family is sitting at a table to my left. I have not told you this before. A lovely baby in pink. Hah! The mother just put her huge white-framed sunglasses on the child. Way too big! But the young toddler is pleased. It is this sense of life that makes this all so perfect. Just look at those grins. They have cool drinks. Tall palms. Sun, almost white. Metal chairs at a café in a real soothing park. And tables, simple ones yes, glossy, almost like mirrors in this bright day.

If I was talking to you on the phone long-distance right now, I'd say, 'God, I feel rich, I'm so lucky,' and I'd drop in the coins.

WHO NOTES: A PARTICULAR PRONOUN, A RESPONSIBILITY

1. Inside

She walks slowly now heading to exit, that same entrance, portal of light to grove described by the walls of the cathedral. Exit, but as if expecting to be stopped, stopped in her path, a tap on her shoulder, a clearing of the throat from the rear, or perhaps, a new thing remembered an excuse like a painting to be admired she would of necessity turn round.
A catch, a run in the stocking.

2. Outside

(for in the break of speech of shifted dissonance) She is now there in the sunlight, warming her cold fingers, gripping her books. The tower rises to the right, the east of her. Almost faith in the archaeology of things, of detail, (the shaking mysterious leaves) in the leaps of time, and thus to surrender to the chain. The chain of light pulls with gentle despair, a persuasion toward the rising. East of her, the sun is relentless, unstoppable, the cathedral tower to admire. The chain of the light.

3. Nether

Now unfolding her composite map and guide to this place into her shoulder bag, she is taking gradual steps backwards very slowly — it is a ridiculous scene: self-absorptive and contrived. The advancement is quick, the pace quickens more (head races) leaning forward such advance, yet stepping quickly backwards in blind. Now blind, running sprint, the movement a dance like gentle persuaded fragments seemingly seamless, taken from narration. In the forest of pillars, the hundreds of pillars of, the jasmine and marble Mezquita, twirling absolute about her the chain in a dervish way. In the archaeology of things she is thinking a handwriting illegible, erased in places, she is surrendering to a faith in things, almost not there.

A tap on the shoulder is all that remains to succeed. Does one continue to the portal? Advance still backwards yet more?

THE LIGHT INSISTENCE

(How is it held, but in the night's occupation of such squares, bench beneath palms, stars over the bell tower.) The walk leads out before and on, in the sun's bristling heat: octopus, green peppers, chopped onions, cut orange sections in the fresh sharp vinagretta, say, this is it that which one comes for; the small hard white of bitten bread-biscuit rings. The small plates, crisp deep-fried anchovies come smartly to the bar, finished, are quickly set away; and (repeat again the phrase, for it threatens even the closed, shaded eye, the uncovered skin) the sun across midday across that heat leading out, leading out before and now again precisely as burn beneath magnifying lens, yet walk on, the direction straight ahead. And yet, a reserve of cool — a bench steady as there in night, this bench, those sunflower seeds, spitting out shells helter-skelter the garbage of papers overfilling the refuse baskets sheltered in the shade of the lacy tropical pines; a stand by Calle Santa Maria de Gracía, readying huge pots boiling away with small snails. Read this, that: the mud of construction how that space provides the way to lose the self on the heels, hard to know whither you're going, then backtrack or thus: 'lose the mind' mind the
way, please; mind

maybe way back huh? Wait. Track past the hot smells from make-shift booth, just happens there (construction site) paprika on spit-roasting chickens maybe tomorrow's supper maybe to find the mind and that is quite a contour, the future's s', passing each step eating the tasty gerund.
The tapping of instruments tap-tap, soundtrack of the foot dance of black heels at the bend precise en route, turning hard on the heels (throwing eyes over this shoulder) glance in descent for home, past the orange trees, past the 'range.' Range = a scope of general idea as place and everything disappearing in a cloud of dust.

In attempts at the dusty scabs of terra cotta church doors, they be used, if ever, if ever then this Church San Rafael? Only what is guess/suspect sculpting at tapas bar the karma which just comes, or as hand pointing at pastry buns filled with fresh sweet cream in the lovely Pastelerias e Cafeteria Serrano — alas, convincingly if one is present to witness the people entering for Mass, opened wide at last.

Even through the hope of open portals, frozen with delay, unmoving before a next walk in some composite plan as one sat over breakfast coffee, a thick tostada with butter and marmalade, map spread out. Spanish cuisine's tapas: small plates a devise of a dance still-ly held in the head, eardrums or clapping say karma unforming the lips thus utter the day with the even cool blunt one names as moon. Slip into mouth. The smart of dumb, sex confusion. The light throbs like a loose bulb through pines insists ever so with tweet-tweet, fresh, passion and thought.

POINTS OF VIEW: THE GARDEN

SEVILLA — 1985-87

Each path, and the passage green revealing the one
pillar, ascendant from clipped hedge & stone bench and

fountain and a sky,
two palms —

    lemons cut in half
    wet with the fountain's
    collect, show in the brush of leaves;

the sun stretching down the corridor
of trees, across the footpath of formidable stone
past the irises, oleanders —

    and the hints of days pass
the mosaic worn smooth,   only rarely a catchable
                                  fragrance,
music of gathered insects,
they after rain.

               (what makes a shade

... the hints of codes or magic skills
in this garden, growing forth
from whose hands & eyes but those of a well-travelled
pilot, a gardener with arduous hoe, a tiny insect
lands upon the printed word.

Moss-covered paths give to moss-covered spout — and tiles
aqueduct
herringboned footpath in cobbled stone, show
decoded animals, to walk and be delightfully
astonished by weakened meaning;

it is lemon caught in mouth that touch acetic temporal measures —
today, tomorrow say, I will speak
you, entering this house gate, chapter beneath lintel,
from one such step it's the whole constructed:
reading through passage:
tomorrow rain forecast:
ticket, finger, bell.

2

Let us follow the emerald along the etched curled current, its cloisonné
where it moves into a kidney-shaped face of ultramarine or cobalt in terrace.
Here and there (yellow exists as background) the movement ties, knots the
black edges, ribbon such gesture, for all donates the decisive stray from path,
surely as cats, wild and at ease beneath garden hedge. Let us trace across
the colours which give here to this dry fountain its early spring glory, a
wetness perhaps it is the signal on the tip of a penis withdrawn. Hues are
the stopping, we stop, it could be even our favourite path towards our most
favourite destination. So, we halt.

3

In every way, can there be discussion — how many places to rest when the
heels have become worn tender and raw with too much pavement, with
sand, with subtle or abrasive intervention.

The fire, perhaps set by the strange flavour in a self's heart and throat, the rancid night-spittle, is hastened into waste when the foot follows the way up one firm step ridged with a glassy ceramic green, in reassuring definition, when turning backwards, only the hat of a stranger is seen above bush or fence and you are admitted through the columns made by cedar trees, smooth, lathe-turned.

A tickle of small ants, that 'ants in the pants' disturbs, nevertheless and ever, o, a picnic then, annoyed by all bestials, or the early too crunchy peach, or a pithy orange scooped from the ground, last year had fallen.

Discussion follows one's camera's shutter, words tingling off the camera strap — in every turn of the cheek versus the opposing checker or goalie, the sunlight reduces as to this gadget, everything, shines everything in turn; and this is reflection and the hand which cups the garden fountain's glory into hands to extinguish that exotic flavour, the fire, that hand processes into the museum, proceeds to the civilization hung on the sturdy, well-guarded walls.

4

Cross-hatch the student artist knows, her look upon the buildings which she knew before but now, crayon in hand is disconsolate. *Cross-hatch,* instruction in technique, and the waiter rushes forth and back, the coffee flies off the tray with its companion glass of tap water, stains the white waiter sleeve, or could have been that collision of two motorcycles at their respective sides, the policeman on one, tossed 'horribly' off to pavement, the busy time rush hour, in French, the word *circulation* no blood, but still the voice, artist, her eyes look up — *cross-hatch,* my dear. It's correct. On this mosaic bench, the blue is finely scratched and forms its corners of ultramarine, a singing sea, windy cliffsides, or sonorous quiet fountain, fine blue lines cross back and forth with plain brown at points of interception: seated. Life is seated, the student once knew, she with her fingers wound too-tightly round her crayon, legs tucked underneath, getting stiff. *Cross-hatch,* my love, days are being x'd-out, now ... the buildings rise lovely before me.

5

I've Got a Secret
 for Frank Davey

'I've Got a Secret' he used to watch on the television, or to be true, heard the track, an ear cupped around the voice of another. There was programme host Garry Moore, and panellists who included Bill Cullen and Henry Morgan.

A diversion or division of the words, the couplet formed the storage in a drum, what be amphora-held, it so silently upon the pedestal, the kitchen window seductive with a Grandma's Apple Pie.

Here and there's not a secret but always the navigable bay, but why? A crab under the rock Mother 'when a little girl' she said, used to clamber for. Neato ... and the angler's secret bait, secret hole what lure did you use, tackle box of metal? The dark how can it penetrate a well-worn path, a manicured lawn, a grand sculpted garden made for royal parties, for the gloss he starts thinking of ... of ... — uv, neato.

Under the shade of fragrant cedars, the more diffuse light of oleander, there are pots of flowers, perhaps two dozen or more, encircling a pool. Barely moving, a dark water, the slender brown leaves, the furry dust of twigs afloat: and a school of goldfish navigate their orange neon through the reflection of trees, who will see them (?) he does, as he once sat before a flickering screen, and listened, volume fixed louder when same Crest Toothpaste (no cavities!), Marlboro Cigarettes (Cowboy!) pumped him, alas, surely pumped him.

THE GOYA

Two cats are facing, will fight. An abandoned wall no
place in particular instinctual the clover between
them say, the vines. There is only grey sky
to support them, their terror.

LOS GALLOS: THE DEEP DISAPPOINTMENT OF THE SEA

SEVILLA — FEBRUARY 1985

she reads,
'or bird in wing, angled,
hurting without flight,'

hurtling, even throwing
she moves across, her hands
 holding day and night in her body
and turns, that swing across
the night, to the singer pointing,
he is pointing at her,
she despises him, and finally marries him.

('It is too much to take, drink
each night your jism, your fucking cum, the take
the moon's cold crescent,
its sharpness is what
I make of you, the guitar
   of night
chorals the pain.')

What you want, demand of how
sex makes the dangerous sword.
This way and that that entry
into the sky, the moon says

drink this last cup, pull here
(like a door) and there.
This is the way passion
is for you. Black hands, arms
twist the branches of desire,
the fish lurking in the hot still
water. Hide your eyes in that
deep forget, the night reach out

to the singer whose voice
is that finger, pointing forever
tempting forever never letting go,
never holding on.
The envoy of a leaf, turn over.

Play the game this way. Square to square,
marble pillar to marble pillar.
Forget the shadow, move one step
closer. I am remembering the way
you demanded. Closer still. The way summer
passed quickly, with warm plates discarded
/herringbone of guilt,
fresh and sweaty on the bedsheets.

Somewhere a cat paws
and yowls

: move
 into the light.

It is the balcony.
The green.
The black jacket
the tie. The white collar
shirt. The belt. The black
pants. The dark stockings
the hard leather shoes. The black
jacket. The undressing. The railing, the bedpost
upon the bed. The clock. The alarm.

The bottle of water upon the night table.
The sign from the café lumines the room.

(a photograph taken)

The black jacket.
The undressing. The black garter.
The dark circles of the breast
the undressing the dark circles of the eyes. The undressing.
It is the balcony. His finger
pointing. It is Romeo and
Juliet. The green vine of
disaster. The black jacket
the black jacket. The black
jacket. The dark jacket. 10, 9, 8.
Finger. Castanets.
The crimson flower in black hair
the edge of red, ($ .15, $ .16)
painted lips the oleander
of night. Black jacket black jacket
black jacket.

The dark plum. The oleander.
You are choking with night. Equinox,
the blade pressed
against the nerve: cool flesh. Dark garden. Vine, garter,
tiles, empty chair in garden.
Tiles covered with moss.
You are cutting bamboo
you are eating ripe banana.
The shadow of fan
upon the white stair. A fan falling.
Like the sound of a swinging chandelier,
the door
it blows shut.

Cross swords. Cross finger.
Cross hands. Green (lime or
melon), red (poppy or blood).
Purple (violet or wine). Orange
(melon or saffron). White lace,
legs and arms so

thin, white. It is the beginning of
painting. The movement of fan.
The deep spoons of sweat, dosage.
The balcony too far, too
close. Dark jacket. Hard
leather shoes. Bound to bed.
Bound to that taste every night.
Prisoned with movement.
The pulsing in and out
the crescent the sky.
Cross hands. Moving, the click
of heels sharp,
beginning in the night, the painting,
starting to sweat,
        breathe.

When the lights go on, the stage is set.
A glaring mid-morning sun makes of the sea
a swathe of crystal codes blacking the form
of small boats. You wipe the dew from your
glasses, the tissue is wet in hands, surrendering
and prisoned in movement, you are
almost home.
A swathe of crystal codes.

THE TAPAS

heat
and sharp perfume of geraniums
the earthy steely scent
of leaves, hairy leaves ...
accusation the spoil of fingers ...

strewn alley is pencil too much
the parallels the strewn   say bone marrow
the parallels distent aches the uneasy of humour
and becomes dark humour with minute advance, the child
   so personal, so autobiographical, snickering, living
   in the background.
Squid — dredged in flour and deep-fried,
marinated anchovies,
grilled kidneys;
stains: gravy, oil ...
In the dusty palm, a pencil is a dwarf

of desire is held, precious cusp
'You're awfully fortunate,' he, others think, the morality
convenient
and it's the complex valley with its almost tolerable heat,
lover and sex-drive all too familiar.

INFACILITY, TOURIST NOTES OF NERJA

So mute. Dumb. The dull throb of no words
to ease with control in a foreign land. Rain pours down.
The hand, throat dumb in the cafés and bars,   signal
 a waiter, pass on.

The rain exploding on the slick terraces, the body
too wet for venture. Only now learning about word,
comma, exclamation, the codified mark.
Dangerous silence — fluent insistence to kill time, fill
tract and colon edged with stupid light and ache
at the point of this weather, cancer.

Here, to escape the snowy Paris winter, demi-tasse
gone cold in Brasserie Canons des Gobelins, to this
cliff-perched town, the wet palm-lined terraces,
ice cream parlours empty. Sipping a café cortado's great fun.

The route of lack,
into the next horizon describes the voice
constants as with light, sun: clear, simple
 gentle: morality the envelope of disappointment,
just serve sweet pudding plainly.

The clatter of the heart as it traces sympatically the photographs to
be and the schedule of train departures.

To the left, a row of palms angle
across, cutting the sky and sea; to the right with equal syncopation
   the pots of scarlet and pink geraniums, the silver
   streetlamps on green posts bristle
   in the daylight glare.
It is 1 p.m. and as dumb. Digits hold place in
the schedule, stretch out from these arches,
the flat white paving, the predictable
green benches, to Balcony of Europe,
cliff-top overlooking the sea, trains fall into the on time or
there's delay.   I am here one stupid word.

The heavy accents spill their escaped vigour,
this town with its colony of grey-haired English, they're all over in
increasingly large percentages here, you see,
their swept doors of their villas ...
brooms, brooms the sense of neatness to all this
verse-y stuff, villas ...

(the edited heart)
rest of longing, longing.

PARTS OF SPEECH

NERJA, SPAIN — FEBRUARY 12, 1985

1

Walk upon a newfound path; a melody upon easy shoulders,
alight, or sand; guess that ultimate note or rest before
the string bass lifts a mediocre air. Walk in a direction
of flowers, the hedgerow — watching the morning glories
and primroses bordering the path, and listen. This
territory from gestural sweet tongue might be, lulla-
bye.

2

'The Pakis are like that. They have no friends. They
use people to get what they want out of them. You know
what I mean? They've got no comradeship. They're like
worms.'

(found path)

3

The fragrant coriander leaf,
the saffron robe, civility is a factory of fresh demand —

how under mid-
night's twinning stars,
and over the dark leagues
of sea, conversations sweep on.

THE PRADO: SIGNS, SECRETS AND SACRED OBJECTS

i.

a) the weight, the density in
   pietà form,   the heavy arm's
    finger in gentle point

    the look of wait
expectant.

  side/glance

    because/ because   thus refers to

b)   the whole weight

minimal given shape
on the floor

attends

to a profile of the hole
(walk around)
/quiet concrete, forged steel
sheens
the angle,
the dense burden
(not forgetful)

  of that / that.

ii.

hold in stone
or clay, the

whiteness, the

cast of light
upon a lover's

   fingers. probing
   what takes flight

          and. Again
takes; that fancy,
a lover's or child's; O, robins, sparrows

all away, sky or simply

'Touch, my love.'

iii.

what is the signal
across the hall?

        (as always

It gives at such distance from
At this entry here we (eyes of the beholder) There is
the book or hand held up, pointing
to the action as if to say
'follow it' the gesture
of moving persona
of moving frames.

And equally could be
there a waste can, say
(it waits)

the sound of metal garbage lids
on pavement in the night;
and voices, words if they are,
undiscerned, behind.

iv.

wait:

who gives the 'news'

v.

you say you hold
to the form in house
— hold love, when boiling
the water for coffee, turning
the gas on just right for simmer, just right move,
hold to the form,
        even so, o.k., a little
stretch it,

just fine.

vi.
   for bpNichol

JUNE 1987

La Magdalena

It is all for Ribera; the Mary, that Magdalena who yet dreams placid upon a worn, well-used skull; so gentle that head placed, so tilted a repose the russet hair, on strand which falls, or is a wire, a message tied to the foot of a pleasant dove held on the head of one. One = dream, a lake turning blue with the early sun, the pulling of ropes, hoisting in the chance, it be the day again: O, it's here again morning, entwined in fingers of clasped hands. Where you or I would utter, 'Silence reins the dream,' we try to describe.

And yet, worn eyes sleep, you want to jump, to sauté, to vault the testicles, prostate's slow throb, that tangled bacterial speech in jism, in discharge, such from there: look, always look at our hands, at our wrists — they age, no? They can't do the solve of emotion of a past love's dark packing her sinuous luggage, the splitting of accumulated belongings, the solve of nothing in particular: look upon the gentle touch on forehead he/she there you can't seem to see whom, smiling ah cool tiny fingers, tiny blonde hair, tiny, tiny, tiny feet on your earlobes no less, so gentle, so small, amazement is fast, is it glue — wet or what sticking now pronoun you seek? It is I calling it is me, sad equivalence, lucky you've forgotten (handy; hey the wrists), the nick of time a b(li)p, something's happening again, a nibble, an insect perhaps — at the ankle, the cool toes at the ear.

vii.

On Wearing a Lampshade

        Just a collar, just on the right side.
Shows the light the way the hand is, tracing, hey
back, is tracing the light (a collar), its fingers to
tell the palm there is a head, a bony skull, under —
under what? The foot, the porch, the leaves ...
the hand; for each blind one, this hand, and each
hand this ticket, each ticket, a lottery, a synonym is
community and be painted on canvas, perimetered with
customs, the modern industrial state, by the gold leaf,
can tell, the traces of the frame-maker, are we losing
tradition, a visceral cord to encyclopedia, to past?

CALLES

1

What last steps:

the empty box
and window of violet blooms
or a stick-figure gent
standing, waiting.

Box is filled with daylight
or flute or space which surrounds
the painted voice,

and she, that large face, that
possible.
Everything: bright red is
bright scarlet around you.

2

The stick figure
looking at the ladder.
He is in the box of light
: or there are pigeons and sparrows
flying forth from the mouth
(of the painter) how he holds
the brush in his teeth
while he throws and glues
hairs directly to canvas.
He is gazing through the window
over Mediterranean blue,
the frame of perched birds and
flowers frame him.
And he paints, leaves
the box, untouched,

he smells the floral breeze.

3

The breeze comes intelligently with everything
you are thinking. You are thinking of the souvenir stone
and the anxious wait
for reunion, the waiting coffee, the tea, the cola, what
to take peaceably under the arms of the vertigo palm.
The heat of this valley, Cordoba sends this sweat.
'I could have brought you flowers,' I address to scent
of dead father, 'I could have charmed
the pants off you,' (to no possible lover in particular).
My brothers and sisters, your children, my father, rub the incense
are holding each other very hard, fiercely to keep in
                    the sympatico,
the maudlin of the occasion, the occasion calls for much
drink, some exquisite cuisine, tuned aha with a fork.
Everyman lies with a pillow of stone under ear. Remember? Conc!
Very hard. The sharp division of memoir, in the dusty field,
the grassy wood, the Alyscamp[24] walk of funereal Rome.
The breeze comes with everything and don't forget to buy postcards,
willingly. A breeze — nope, a bouquet of daisies and freesias.
We will take planes all of us to Marseilles, train it to Arles
and walk that you know.
Picnic, it's the idea of fun.

TWO IN BARCELONA

IN A SLEEP

Cat is sleeping underneath
your hope. Somewhere inside
the chamber you are small,
have a dress on. The stars
cast light upon the canvas.
A little man is approaching
you with a hat-box. He is frequent
he, carrying the choice — to be
strong, or feeble and attack
with red bricks even so,
that red blood flows.

THE CLOTHES

The bird figure in the mouth.
The fish bones in the throat.
Light fills this room, while outside
laundry hangs from dark balconies
: there are sox, there are
towels, voices fill, as if
meals around tables, with sepia flavours,
and oil, strong knuckles wrapped around
spoons. Across the sea, which fills
this afternoon window is death
of your father and how you sought
release through laughter /a balcony is
now filling with small birds and a
solitary one is perched on a wooden
pole. It looks like it is at aqua sea
it is framed across the iron
grate, and you almost can reach
out, through the bars; reach
from the balcony, and
come home.

FURTHER

The sharp spice smell of rosemary stiffens the body,
more so the cock, this one; and under
such sweet breeze, oranges fall, into damp
winter lawns (they will rot). The cock is too big,
getting bigger yet against the slacks with the touch
of goat hair and hind leg and new cheese under hand.

                     The radio wrenches, the sudden
but protracted dispersion of small pebbles, the Sevillanas[25]
and ads
are the marble floor, sandy in the sleeproom opened
by the sturdy hostel keys.
In corridor, the door, another one yet, to the washroom proffers
the gentle soapy smells so delicate a sex, intact the unbronzed
body arrived by chance maybe in a bus en route intimate
such this, so much stranger ...

FUGUE IN FIGUERAS

This afternoon visits as Spain, but visits as memory from contours and hues of its map, a concept afar is now, as Toronto. As such heat to take for instance on the hand when it is a visor to light. The glare of this walk — uncomfortable, dispirited — and dust and exhaust and loud music of passing cars and the repose in it all, to find hot quiet sectors. The muscular action of the heart seduces without intent the mind, as image bleeds from the learned potent of speech. As inert as this air is Spain. When one grasps onto 'for instance' in parole, situation freed from the general, it is particular as hot and sunny as arrival in Figueras in Catalán such as this, Saturday in summer — with the lethargy of shops and intermittent dark flies; and sugared sweets of a baker's window. A loved one too is product here in suite, for she too arrived companion into that Figueras flame; but now gone, her absence strokes a visit of one's previous tour there, lugging baggage from train, this afternoon's oil-mark circle from sweets left, an hour forgotten, this afternoon indeed visits as Spain, but it is a changed inert air of itself, own ventricle, this quiet sector, content, potent of speech.

IN CADAQUES
> *for Mother and Alan*

There are those fishy smells again. It is as if Mother has baked fish, cooked the rice, like she has so many times in past. The screen window is torn and that almost metallic scent of geraniums lingers on my fingers. Why are the kitchen lights on when fading sunlight casts its easy glow across this land, poking past yellowed blinds into our house? We did not really ever own this house.

When I speak like this, when I think like this, the faces grow big and traverse the waters; and even the sight of shoreline — white Catalán stucco above the breakwall sharpens the mind with two distinct sights: home and not-home; hand and not. That clear, that close. I feel upon fingertip.

There are these stony alleyways, the streets of this village, here sharp-cobbled to the espadrille feet, and point — there was 'Al, let's play catch in the lane (by our house)' and this is about two brothers growing up, always the three years' apart: the torn screen window through which the smells of salmon and mackerel pass, he too would remember. 'You call this a playground?' The grounder, the hardball took a bad hop on a pebble, hit me in the jaw, I cried, what do you want? I was a kid. Then the airborne chestnut leaves, the broken bottles and oil-soaked rags. A lane as is we always pass everywhere, so much. So much the smells of that fish, in the small hotels on Costa Brava shore where lunch plates have just been set to dry. Stop walking, rest briefly at this vantage point. Touch fingertip to thumb, sea plants to breakwall. One looks not for shapeful beginnings head or tail. The face of my Mother simply, that regard across the bay. Through the tendencies caught unaware in the passing lane, the clutch of speech nearly uttered, broadens the heart.

CADAQUES (II)

Take the gusts from green mountains.
Wear the curve of the bay road
around your waist. A sash to your
taste it is hanging in a shop for pesetas. A bell
rings once in the sea.

Garlic, sardines, blood sausage and hot
grilling pans: cover the nose
and ears.
Open the mouth.

Again arriving from Figueras by bus,
those hairpin turns — ascending then descending
over mountain road;
in the pocket of it / pitch of tires upon pavement,
burning feet; the turn into dusk.

Take the gusts from green mountains.
Wear the curve of the bay road
around your waist. A sash to your
taste it is hanging in a shop for pesetas. A bell
rings once in the sea.

'Since that time I came here when I was small with my parents,
it was by accident too, I've thought it my favourite place
in the world.' Her voice now so distant, drums the present
to the ear.
And now back from the shore, on a narrow street, Casa Anita,
the kitchen's hot smoke blows through plastic-ribbon curtains.

Garlic, sardines, blood sausage and hot
grilling pans; cover the nose
and ears.
Open the mouth.

Taste of saliva only a repression,
disguises the bloodied fish or throbbing
butcher-readied pig. And out over sea
is that taste for re-enactment or repetition,
favourite place be that pork-heart, air sanguine
of the eve.

Take the gusts from green mountains.
Wear the curve of the bay road
around your waist. A sash to your
taste it is hanging in a shop for pesetas. A bell
rings once in the sea.

And now,
shadowy skiffs float moored beneath the ease
of the stars; blonde cat seeks the dark stench, scratching
for fleas; it swings its collar, its tail, O,

a garlic hangs heavily in
the heart.

Take the gusts from green mountains.
Wear the curve of the bay road
around your waist. A sash to your
taste it is hanging in a shop for pesetas. A bell
rings heavily in
the heart.

ITALY

THE WHITE, THE RED, THE BLUE

Is it this to walk with another, take that other
up the steep white steps, over that referrent
sound of tides, the red: and the white steps
mark this entry to the telling streets.
Is it that one walks with anything but the bad odour,
the bile float through cornea and lid up the steep
white steps, past the red stockings drying across
the windy balconies, and there to be directly facing
the bright blue doors of wood.

And yet, it is the still,
the framed and hung painting's sure-point,
more emphatic with corner signature:
it is the small white boat
the child is missing, you have aged childless
and the deep blue heralds as knock at that door
and chipping paint
the deep blue engine silent astern
the small white boat,
pinioned or painted with the depth of the sea.

&

THE PITCH

Clouds veil for certain an uncertain
this half-moon, to wit its fullness
a reminder hanging with castanets
or tabla;

and beating rain a reminder
when too with stars in same scene shine
that dark

pitcher
inside deeply banged.

A blackening pitch and the falling
 forward into confidence and be not the moon's
image or voice any more but casual,

the pages torn from the calendar and where
is it going

or now stars.

DOMENICO

Domenico. Peacoat; dark tan. Electrician, former seaman. Resident in Amalfi; now out of work. If I was to give you a fact sheet, a CV, that much I would give. 'Attention: all media.' And now, little does remain in my hands, of our talk together, walking the shore, the curving road of this town. First in one direction, then past the main square to the other — out upon the pier where he pointed out the lights of Minori, then Atrani, his home, a kilometre away. Under a sky, he cut the line where speech is thrown out to sea (ahoy!) and comes back, still dry. And up through this town in mixture of Italian, English, French and gesture — he led me through the Valley of the Mulli pointing out the paper mills, older, he told, than any left in Europe.

I am not sure whether he or I heard the usual Duomo bells, that night. Put out your hands say, spread them a foot, a foot and a half maybe: call this Italy, call this Campania. And then look, where he is taking me out upon the pier (can one believe guidebooks or stories by others who talk of those who will steal one's money and passport?)
he pushes me into
the Tyrrhenian Sea, taking my possessions. He jumps in, Domenico, after me. We are saying goodnight. I climb the stairs to my pensione. We are saying goodbye. 'Much work for electricians in Canada?' he'd probed. We are saying goodbye. My back is loaded. I am reading an Italian phrase book. Domenico, a CV slash mark on his face, begins speaking, in the moonlight, the Tyrrhenian tides.

SHE: TRAGEDY SET IN CAMPANIA

It is because what you say, could
/what could happen; I would divine her
here, this day this story. Because I could say
she can be this; or that as well, free, let me
make her look in ways she wants — Oh!
So douce, or if it pleases her, broad-shouldered
speak, as they say, from the hip, cigarette
at the corner of her lips. Who dispenses these pleasures
of dressing as she wishes, which is
scarecrow or Madonna or Venus
in this plain grass field? The energies, a satin fuchsia
    slipper, Oh! Cinderella!
    A man's smoking-jacket — the structure built

        into these stones,
circle, or angular column, a vestibule a
theatre; in this sun, lizards
dart across these ruins. are darting,
perfume of small oranges

the fingernail digging sharply into the bitter peel
citric juices upon raw of unprotected
skin of my thumb.

        She performs for me?
        How long this theatre, these rain-
        washed
            columns   to stand?

        angles,
        measures, the architectural plans
        on parchment,
        the thirst.

THE FRAME

PAESTUM, CAMPANIA

Is it then to look from upon high
the form, plan of things
as they were: the past tense; verb
in all its purity, cut from dense
weighty rock. Or there is that closer
sight of dry grass
weed and lizard touching the fallen column,
the pedestal still poised under sky.
10 square-cut boulders the foundation
for what everyday forms
into life and yet, I too young and yet
even too new to this continent
to make in concept
or skeleton
of these hardened facts.

and

Even before these rocks were cut, the sand,
the life of animals swept forth in

the sea, the sea winds,
the winds across land. Language, when I say
for instance, 'I love you,' anoints this prehistory
renewed, this dust coating my palms; in service,
in liturgy co-accident here where water flows,
there is rain enough here
to soak a grey land, the lizards of this column,
for
another coming.

2

To look, bend down
crouch. To meet this theatre of stone
face to face. The mouth with fruit taken
from terrace grove. To sow
seeds in a city lawn
the moral question posed by slugs
: at arm's reach, the insect-bomb
we hold on the shelf, that preparedness
before what we must face.

MUSIC OF THE TWO WORLDS: ABRUZZO

Past the snow, these mountain foot-
hills, there are houses, stone and golden,
pheasants hens too running across the yards,
in late morning light.

Train headed for Umbria province,
a traveller's spoon unfolded, sandwiches of dried
ham, mountain sheep's cheese, bananas, raw endives
white and pale yellow, apples — each mouthful
cut with a knife ah.

Loud. Transistor radio romantic symphony or what
is loud in one ear, the knot
of another's
pleasure
uh, violins, bags are stuffed with food, good
preparations, baggage — sweet round cakes
powdered sugar in cellophane, that crackling,
packaged sound.

Or then, a pulling of hair ehh, slap,
slap all they are all laughing these
teens so much, the: so much
is not tranquil, the speeding
train;

'Do you want some of this: some of
that?' And chew, (the delicious knot of pleasure)
(   )

chew   along the steel
tracks, rusted cable   now this electric
guitar solo and now a green hill for Battisti,
song from that radio

and silence (the hills already we have
passed long ago the running
of hens farm birds

and that clack-clack of train tracks, we're always on,
always there
before it begins again.
The cello' bags they're

opening.

UMBRIAN SPRING

past, beneath the arch spaces black marble
pillars make, the cracked stone.
nun awaits the passing clouds
too cold in this damp winter air.

Are her hands folded, failing hands,
marked, scribbled with light,
pin sharp in the glass dark
secret, under the wooden doors,
    protected from day?

The paintings overhead, the gold gilt
weighs too strongly, yet not
of a fool's gold. Fauna, flora their recension
to cumulous and blue
(Forbearance Lesson).

He looks too at so many hands, palms
upturned with humble want,
like the beggars who crouch the table
of alarm.

Or she/he who reads quiet-
ly the words softened as speech
in whispers by a bush,
a melting light upon ice.
    For he knows,
the way the fingers
need not harden, remain to give
to the leather of book, its background
its context of allusion, reference
to the spoken to the speechless parole.

Not the *gold* or caned choir stalls
the animals, faces upon the hands where hands

be placed.
Mark with such hands
in font of eyes ...

The two windows symmetric in the apse, the
leaded light, grey which entered, giving steady,
silver curve to each carved bench, like waves
frozen as memory, suggesting what he
had planned to do, but, he was still,
rooted, his hand stroking finding the
slope of each curve of polished wood.
That silver in eyes, would never
come to hands, an uplifted palm,
ready; he be ready.

The neat rows of arches over marble pillars
down the sides of the church, everything,
about arch, the way it made breath
shrink and distend with each
stroke. Faster, then slower. He would look up,
and see the steady candles the melted wax.
Chairs piled in a corner,
the triangle of light beneath an arch.
Clutch heart, or head   firewood?

The smell of wood.

You will find this next again somewhere else
and later, in some other poem,

past the door,
into the courtyard, the pink stone still fresh
and bright, hot to the touch,
      the rectangular opening, into the (Via
                              Cavour)
the raised arms of trees, giving passage.

STOFFA DI FIRENZE

FIRENZE — MARCH 1985

What is guarded in gentle hands. Wrap these cold hands in fabric, nearly but not. In kneel the gentle kiss upon lordly feet.

The sound of the dustbin: metal. These cold stone tile floors a caretaker sweeps before the first mass.

What is guarded in gentle hands. Or gentler. The habit of light and dark, that worn each day. The habit of word its join in repose with palms or knees; or mountain fire, cinders in a March woodlot or single white taper steadfastly aglow. A race, race to flame, clasped hands. Pain, sorrow or humility — are these those things which wrought tender repose in those days? The robe which at night veils the moon in silence, the breeze which moves the curtains through the open channel of night.

There is a crucial balance, cock and hen set before contact, here, daylight that frost, that grey luminescent passing through this church, crossing; small amber and yellow flame on gold candlesticks. When the self is alone, it moves steps too gingerly towards greed, towards impious self-knowledge, wanting forcefully the determined humble form of a Renaissance sculpture housed in apse, classic and now an object of prayer and peace in the eyes of parishioners.

Here in the glass case, the burlap, the torn habit worn by San Francesco when he received the wounds on the Mount, torn, habit which by knowledge is repeated, again and again, and mumbling. The sound of the dustbin: metal. These cold stone tile floors.

The burlap, torn habit worn by San Francesco when he received the wounds on the Mount, torn, habit which by knowledge is repeated, again and again, and mumbling catches up confuses itself upon a tongue-twisting path, again and again, repetition ...

One after another the sound of cars outside, the morning traffic along the paved banks of the Arno.

ENGLAND

WALK ALONG THE WYE
  for Geoffrey Goss

This cup on table

in hand

an accent

this hand

an accident

an act.

This cup on table   in hand
an accident   this hand

an accident,

 a tract.

*

BROCKWEIR, WALES

That breeze which takes away
the breath   away the mind
such strobe
those violet blooms, pointillis'on hillsides
measure against a come-upon post.

                        Where we stand. Station.
The silent joust, the pedestal up

            comes robed in dark ink
        (that's night's descent).

                    But this hand
        could be sprayer of this field
                by delicate muscle
the return which comes be breath, inspired
berry bush to prune,   or tangled wire.

To pray when cars pass in a faith of choice,
the TV or not;
when the city is full of mumble a 'Chinatown,
downtown, fast pizza and hip —
rings the zero alarm.

   Attend:
        a porch is what one
        remembers on

            on

                        the dew worm   in grass.

A CATHEDRAL SQUARE

GLOUCESTER — MAY 25, 1995

A shapely procession.
Cold flat stones,
beneath

fan-vaulted corridors:

this is what be forgetting
that voice is about
the walk, to say
'walk on stone,' already
the graves worn smooth,
                        they are dry and warm.

      that fatal —

the soft undulating cast
chambers overcast light
this spring.

We are as if living
forever in a cloister crows, cut grass to scent,

forsythia grows there
is neolithic, there is
 Norman stone

voice forever for you walk in square; glory
wear, the cloister refrain

in chorus grace

you have there a wooden bench commemorate,
it is singular
it is waiting for you there.

*

GLOUCESTER

I say nothing of scanning up,
of tourists caught with cameras
in eye, to capture stained glass,
that regal sky.

  Only the traffic! Saturday shoppers outside —

Of the line of book upon books
on choir stalls /red, green, black
anthems, hymns to sing
marked pages in creation or
now by pencil light;

and there too, the cushions needlepointed
to sign as well fair are,
the worn tapestries, they chronicle the time,
place, that manner of breath
manner:

colour

    in (dif
   fer
      ence)

   blood   grass   sky and wine
we are, it is fitting always

      as in picnic
of choice

our hesitants be nurtured
in the feeding light.

BIBURY WIND

The heart upon this river
flawless, leaves
no lint.
Moving, that stride;
that swam, neck
arched into water: (swan)
green feed, so, smoothly water's flow
duck's smooth slide from flight too,
to float. The heart

upon this river road (and in a van,
driver drinks tea from a flask; a cotton
shirt, fully buttoned, loose) arrives
summer wind, vents a chill.

CATHEDRAL SQUARE

When you come singing the cool odd verse,
or scan rá-tra-lá, you scan from a seat upholstered
with needlepoint ensign and there's the surety,
and there's the edged coloured glass which teaches
and do you then keep that remarkable tune tra-lá?
Sometimes a teaching be unnoticed, is a placid corner
where we relax a few minutes from shopping this is
the church and notice, notice that we rest beneath
such sculpted special walls. Beans on toast, veal
egg and ham pie, a gammon ploughman's, and the Moles
Club Disco and natural cosmetics like bayberry
and at the tea shop, nicely set for 'Morning Coffee'
Kenco or *Rombout's Premium*, the excavation of certain
materials: message sticks, property marks, tallies on bark,
oracle bones.

The fan-vaults overhead comfort, thus footsteps
they tread softly now these paths, the paths
we go and the rehearsals, notes of scale they they
fragrant fragrant fall from
a loft, the heights
it composed it be composed well it composes is
well,
and it will.

What else? Look around, the *Noonday Organ Recital for Shoppers*.
'Where To Go, What To See' it is written
on this tourist board *'Mini-Guide'* and I am peckish
we join here the all of us and the guide's coaxing,
and menu after menu posted on windows
windows where we pass.

THE BRITISH MUSEUM: PRELIMINARIES

To stand up placed in walk, the speech does beckon
from a walking-stick; the eyes where placed
in gander.

*

Black basalt and a mythological text
(710 B.C.): Shabaka Stone has been inscribed
to presence a content of pressure. Damaged,
it was used as a millstone and remains
that for eternity.

AS IN SNOW OR STRATEGY OR CONQUEST: THE BRITISH MUSEUM

1

he who stands and looks
pointing

/
'Who's speaking?' (please) that voice is

— stairs. pointed finger
figure

walking.
'Who's speaking, please?'

who is writing
on the treble
that trestle of crossing place
that trembling
  speech
trembling
stream.

2

he's giving speeches
he's given to speech
        again
the tin can, rolling down the street
kick the can
kick in the ass
he's given to he's
giving it all
away.

MERCHANT OF GREAT RUSSELL STREET, LONDON

Hands raised now, Allah!

   Keep such hands addressed,
   palms flat, to the surface
   of this round table of alarm. Lift open in this ring
   of waking light,
   the teapot's lid, the lovely single flower in china blue vase
   and cream cakes or teacakes with currants all
   the properties of habit high tea and
   Allah! Allah! Steam: tannic, caffeinated,
   steady sure hands
   walk that distance, lift the crepuscular lid
   to the vaporous laurel and basil, where the English
   on holiday tour and revelation escape
   no central heating — cottages, flats,
   to sunny Iberian coasts,
   it is this warm.

   The illuminated books or the hand of cantaor
   kept by our sides, frequent hip-pocket-visitors,
     as we move across the brittle tortoise-shell floor, ouch
       of it all ...

     'Will you chance, will you — uh, sorry — I meant, meant
     dance with me?' one asks fearfully. And she

   be seated by her Schweppes, a tonic with ice and it says
   'Fizzz ...' can
   break this heart o' mine.

The beer is that drawn of night, napkin
is this portal of a bar, the ham-leg from Jabugo
the cutting hour of my life, tastes always
of tradition, of hope of
cured (it was sick?) in evergreen mountain air, my life,
sir innkeeper, my life, like flash-cards in my mouth,
so says the subject, hands leafing the table of contents
so ringing from Omega sleep,
leaving the shelves of the singing merchant of antiquarian
books and ribbons   medals,   tea-stained teeth,
someone niftily antiquarian is I believe,
crocheting, crotchety in the back room of London Town.
I shall check my pulse now, this interruption, a charm so be
I call this dizzy, this whimsy you've come
serious with me, so serious! Allah! Let's beat it back
onto the street.

TENSE EMERGENCY

Who wants to speak, now, of yesterday
the day before yesterday, infinitum the day's advance >the morning
                                         paper —

or write
about the curiosities attacking the fringe and overleaf
of desire, the costume affixed to unclear passion,
     the pick-rot of teeth on a Venetian Carnival mask
there is sweet taste to be had, and delightful porcelain.
The savour left in mouth, the long finish once sugar,
  to cavity or yeast,
 then sour bile from cough, poor vintage
aggravation
then sweet longing dear,
the petals hang dry and fragile, spoke to you on the phone ...
                 you mentioned Venice occupied your heart, a
potpourri sachet of tea-rose.

The spray of mica dust on papyrus,
the imprint one's, makes to others
in a subway crowd, a, athletics,
isotonics the bodies we build keep fit, away
  from the AIDS, the cancer, the trough
we want charms, strips of silver,
polish, polish won't tarnish
sit down and write a will,
it is strong desire to succeed
tell you sugar, the right words, be successful in life, make my folks
and friends proud, beads
to assure
hands, un-
 steady
do you love me, love me? just a kid, just TV, TV.

ROTHKO ROOMS[26]

To stand here at attention, and
stare, unblinking at that
for which we have wandered:

Quiet fiery gate, or the zero. Landscape
which is the tongue's tiger heat, heart burning with
desert, or these sheet-metal strips, side
by side the oxidized oxidized;
 the changeability
of the climate
in the natural state of affiliation,
teaming affectation, the painterly
would sable upon the phrases one does not
have to utter to loved ones,
to dead ones.

BLACK OR MAROON / A SPARROW'S GREY

each perch is a seed or fallen crumb remembered in
the winged stillness
the peck of each in the wind
twig to twig the
changing face, twig-face and crumb-smile
the frontispiece
and salutation
the end

the end of a wind's book
bye-bye.

ENDNOTES

ENDNOTES

BOOK I

1. *Le Figaro:* A Paris newspaper.
2. *Belons, claires, speciales:* Types of oysters.
3. *Shoyu:* Soy sauce.
4. *Harissa:* Hot pepper sauce in North African cuisine.
5. *Gîte:* House for vacation rental.
6. *Cortado:* Espresso coffee with small amount of hot milk.

BOOK II

7. *Granita:* Italian version of dish of stirred ice-slush, usually flavoured with lemon or espresso coffee.
8. *Exterior Façade:* Much of this text is from a tourist information leaflet from Perugia.
9. *Secret:* Two nights, Verona: Somehow, the memory of Shakespeare's couple entered this romantic evening's text.

BOOK III

10. When I arrived in Paris in the autumn of 1984, I had just missed a concert by *Elisabeth Caumont*. Over the years, I followed her career as she became a prominent figure upon the European jazz scene. A few months before the publication of *Aqueduct*, during another return to Paris, I was able to see and hear her on one of her rare gigs in Paris. It was again in the 14th arrondissement, not far from where l'Écume stood. We chatted briefly, and now she will have my little memoir poem she inspired. And, needless to say, thirteen years later she has become a remarkable chanteuse.
11. *Branché:* Trendy.
12. *LePen:* Jean-Marie LePen, leader of the ultra right-wing political party *Le Front National*.

13. The phrase *'colour of speech'* is taken from the title of a book by Lola Lemire Tostevin.

14. *Lovely blueness:* In *Lovely Blueness*, the painting by American Sam Francis.

15. *Auvergnat:* From the Auvergne region of Southern France.

16. *Robert Filiou:* Artist from the historic Fluxus Movement in France.

17. *Scene i:* A newspaper item about singer Michael Jackson thinking about being 'frozen' to 'prolong' life would not let go of this poem.

18. *Samaritaine:* Paris department store.

19. *Christo:* Artist whose widely-known projects have included wrapping 'sites' such as the Pont Neuf.

20. *Jacques Rancourt:* Founder and director of the *Festival Franco-Anglais de poésie*. In the course of this poetry translation festival during 1985, I came upon the work of Algerian writer Mohamed Dib. This text is based on my own translation of his poem.

21. *Master Fauré:* Composer Gabriel Fauré was Master of Music at the Church of the Madeleine.

22. *Duende:* This irrepressible character, goblin throughout Spain, is in fact more like life and death, a snicker, the heart of the spirit of flamenco in Andalusia.

23. *Aware:* Japanese word which can mean: pity, compassion, to have pity; sad; to have a poetic sensibility. Sometimes used to characterize a profound but quiet sense in a work of Japanese art.

24. *Alyscamp, in Arles, France:* Roman burial site. Walk which has inspired poets and artists. Van Gogh and Gauguin have particularly been associated with this site.

25. *Sevillanas:* A traditional form of music from Andalusia.

26. *Rothko Rooms:* The last two poems were inspired by the major exhibition of paintings by American Mark Rothko at the Tate Gallery in London during the summer of 1987.

Gerry Shikatani of Montréal is a poet, prose-writer, and text-sound artist who has published and performed his work across Canada and internationally for over 20 years. His documentary film about language, produced and directed by filmmaker Jess Nishihata, is in the final stages of completion. At the same time, *Opening Series*, a collaborative film work with the internationally acclaimed experimental filmmaker Phillip Hoffman of Ontario, has been screened/performed last year and continues in process.

Born in Toronto, Gerry Shikatani is a Nikkei (of Japanese ancestry). His publications include *1988 — Selected Poems and Texts, 1973-1988* (Aya Press/The Mercury Press) and *A Sparrow's Food* (Coach House Press). He was also co editor of *Paper Doors. an anthology of Japanese-Canadian poetry*, a landmark work in the literature of Multicultural Canada. *Lake and Other Stories*, a book of short stories (The Mercury Press) will be published in fall 1996.